TO
To\
Te'

2

L
are
a

MAGAZINE

delicious.

FOOD FOR FRIENDS

HarperCollins*Publishers*
77–85 Fulham Palace Road,
Hammersmith, London W6 8JB
www.harpercollins.co.uk

First published by HarperCollins*Publishers* 2009

10 9 8 7 6 5 4 3 2 1

© Seven Publishing Group Ltd 2009

A catalogue record of this book is available from the British Library

ISBN-13   978-0-00-729255-4

Printed and bound in China by South China Printing Co.

delicious. MAGAZINE
FOOD FOR FRIENDS

Edited by Debbie Major

Magazine Editor
Matthew Drennan

HarperCollins*Publishers*

contents

introduction

When it comes to entertaining, there is the formal dinner party; the casual, swing by for a bite to eat; or the cosy drop in and we'll crack open a bottle and spoil ourselves with something nice. However you do it, there's nothing as satisfying as cooking – or showing off a bit – for good friends.

In **delicious.** magazine, we offer a range of fantastic ideas for entertaining, and this book brings you the best of all worlds. In the opening chapter – starters and small bites – you'll find recipes such as spiced prawn poppadums and sesame yogurt dip with flatbreads for casual evenings when a nibble and drink kick off the evening nicely. For a smarter affair, there are 'proper' starters such as chicken liver parfait or great twists on classics like coronation prawn and mango cocktail.

The chapters on comfort food and al fresco fare will come to your rescue whether it's a winter Sunday roast or summer barbecue with great dishes such as crispy crackling roast pork with roasted apples or barbecued leg of lamb with tomato and mint salsa.

There are also great main courses for those who love meat, fish, and vegetarian meals and a special chapter dedicated to side dishes and salads, which can be a meal in themselves. And, of course, no evening of great food would be complete without the perfect dessert. Whatever the season, there's a pudding to suit your mood from sparkling summer fruit jellies to winter warmers such as mango puddings with chilli syrup.

Matthew Drennan
delicious. Magazine Editor

Conversion tables

All the recipes in this book list only metric measurements (also used by Australian cooks). The conversions listed here are approximate for imperial measurements (also used by American cooks).

Oven temperatures

°C	Fan°C	°F	Gas	Description
110	90	225	¼	Very cool
120	100	250	½	Very cool
140	120	275	1	Cool
150	130	300	2	Cool
160	140	325	3	Warm
180	160	350	4	Moderate
190	170	375	5	Moderately hot
200	180	400	6	Fairly hot
220	200	425	7	Hot
230	210	450	8	Very hot
240	220	475	9	Very hot

Weights for dry ingredients

Metric	Imperial	Metric	Imperial
7g	¼oz	425g	15oz
15g	½oz	450g	1lb
20g	¾oz	500g	1lb 2oz
25g	1oz	550g	1¼lb
40g	1½oz	600g	1lb 5oz
50g	2oz	650g	1lb 7oz
60g	2½oz	675g	1½lb
75g	3oz	700g	1lb 9oz
100g	3½oz	750g	1lb 11oz
125g	4oz	800g	1¾lb
140g	4½oz	900g	2lb
150g	5oz	1kg	2¼lb
165g	5½oz	1.1kg	2½lb
175g	6oz	1.25kg	2¾lb
200g	7oz	1.35kg	3lb
225g	8oz	1.5kg	3lb 6oz
250g	9oz	1.8kg	4lb
275g	10oz	2kg	4½lb
300g	11oz	2.25kg	5lb
350g	12oz	2.5kg	5½lb
375g	13oz	2.75kg	6lb
400g	14oz	3kg	6¾lb

Liquid measures

Metric	Imperial	Aus	US
25ml	1fl oz		
50ml	2fl oz	¼ cup	¼ cup
75ml	3fl oz		
100ml	3½fl oz		
120ml	4fl oz	½ cup	½ cup
150ml	5fl oz		
175ml	6 fl oz	¾ cup	¾ cup
200ml	7fl oz		
250ml	8fl oz	1 cup	1 cup
300ml	10fl oz/½ pint	½ pint	1¼ cups
360ml	12fl oz		
400ml	14fl oz		
450ml	15fl oz	2 cups	2 cups/1 pint
600ml	1 pint	1 pint	2½ cups
750ml	1¼ pints		
900ml	1½ pints		
1 litre	1¾ pints	1¾ pints	1 quart
1.2 litres	2 pints		
1.4 litres	2½ pints		
1.5 litres	2¾ pints		
1.7 litres	3 pints		
2 litres	3½ pints		
3 litres	5¼ pints		

UK–Australian tablespoon conversions

1 x UK or Australian teaspoon is 5ml

1 x UK tablespoon is 3 teaspoons/15ml

1 Australian tablespoon is 4 teaspoons/20ml

starters and
small bites

Spiced prawn poppadoms

These mini poppadoms are easy to make and have a real zing about them. Perfect as a party nibble with drinks.

MAKES ABOUT 30
READY IN 35 MINUTES

300g fresh cooked and peeled
   medium-sized prawns
1 tbsp tandoori curry paste
5 tbsp low-fat natural yogurt
Finely grated zest of 1 lime,
   plus lime wedges to garnish
   (optional)
Small handful of chopped fresh
   coriander, plus extra leaves
   to garnish
100g bag mini poppadoms
Mango chutney, to serve

1. Drain the prawns of any liquid, then pat dry with plenty of kitchen paper.

2. In a bowl, mix the curry paste, yogurt, lime zest and coriander together, then season to taste. Stir in the prawns to coat evenly in the mixture and set aside for 15 minutes to allow the flavours to develop.

3. Take about 30 whole poppadoms from the bag. Divide a small amount of the spiced prawns among each, then transfer to serving plates. Top each with a small blob of mango chutney and a fresh coriander leaf. Garnish each plate with lime wedges, if you like. Serve straight away.

Variation You don't always have to stick to using tandoori curry paste for these little bites; korma, rojan josh or laksa curry pastes would also all work well.

Thai fish cakes on lemongrass sticks

Serve these with a sweet chilli and lime dipping sauce as a light starter, or as an appetizer with drinks.

MAKES 20
READY IN 25 MINUTES

300g cod fillet, boned and
  skinned
200g raw shelled prawns
5 spring onions, chopped
2 tbsp Thai green curry paste
1 tsp grated fresh root ginger
2 tsp fish sauce
1 tbsp light soy sauce
Handful of chopped fresh
  coriander
10 long lemongrass sticks,
  halved lengthways
2 tbsp olive oil
150ml sweet chilli sauce
Juice of 1 lime, plus wedges
  to serve

1. Put the cod, prawns, spring onions, curry paste, ginger, fish and soy sauces and coriander into a food processor and process until broken down but not completely smooth.

2. Using slightly wet hands, shape this mixture evenly into 20 oval-shaped fish cakes. Thread each one on to the fatter end of the halved lemongrass sticks.

3. Preheat the grill to Medium. Brush a grill rack with a little oil, and put the fish cakes on it in one straight line. Lay a piece of foil across the bare lemongrass sticks to stop them burning. Brush the fish cakes with the remaining oil and pop under the grill for 10 minutes, turning halfway, until cooked through and golden. Transfer to a serving platter.

4. Meanwhile, mix the sweet chilli sauce and lime juice in a little bowl and serve as a dipping sauce, with lime wedges.

★ DELICIOUS. TIP If you can't get lemongrass, you can instead use wooden or bamboo skewers. Soak them in cold water for 30 minutes first, to avoid burning.

Pastry squares with goat's cheese, pesto and tomato

Make these simple snacks in advance, and then bake them as your guests arrive so they are served hot and crispy.

MAKES 20
READY IN 30 MINUTES

375g pack ready-rolled puff pastry
75g soft goat's cheese
120g fresh green or red pesto sauce
20 cherry tomatoes, a mixture of red and yellow, halved
Small handful of fresh basil leaves, to garnish

1. Preheat the oven to 200°C/fan 180°C/gas 6. Line 2 baking sheets with non-stick baking paper.

2. Unroll the pastry and cut it into 20 squares, each measuring 5cm. Place them on the baking trays and top each one with a little goat's cheese, ½ teaspoon pesto and 2 cherry tomato halves. You can cover and chill them at this point, if you wish.

3. Bake for 15–20 minutes until the pastry is cooked, crisp and golden. Push any tomatoes that have fallen off back on to the pastries and transfer them to serving trays. Serve hot or cold, garnished with fresh basil leaves.

Variation Try making these with tapenade, a black olive paste from the south of France, instead of pesto.

Chicken liver parfait with French bread toast

This smooth-style paté spread over French bread toast is a perfect light starter. Delicious served with a few salad leaves.

SERVES 8
TAKES ABOUT 1¼ HOURS, PLUS COOLING AND OVERNIGHT CHILLING

325g unsalted butter, melted and cooled slightly, plus a little extra for greasing

500g chicken livers, trimmed

1 garlic clove, crushed

2 tbsp brandy

A small pinch each of ground nutmeg, cloves, cinnamon and allspice

1 baguette, sliced and toasted, to serve

Onion marmalade, to serve

1. Preheat the oven to 110°C/fan 90°C/gas ¼. Grease 8 x 100ml ramekins with melted butter.

2. Put the livers, garlic, brandy and spices into a food processor. Season with white pepper and 1 teaspoon of salt and blend for 1 minute. With the machine still running, add 225g of the melted butter. Press through a fine sieve into a bowl.

3. Divide the mixture among the ramekins and cover each with buttered foil. Put in a small roasting tin and pour in hot water to come halfway up the sides of the ramekins. Cook for 45 minutes or until just set. Remove from the tin and cool. Remove the foil and cover each ramekin with cling film. Chill overnight.

4. The next day, melt the remaining butter in a small pan. Leave to cool and settle for 10 minutes, then pour the clear butter into a clean bowl and discard the sediment. Pour a thin film over each parfait and chill until set. Serve with the toast and onion marmalade.

Sesame yogurt dip with flatbreads

This traditional dip often has a North African spice blend
called zahtar sprinkled over it – do try it, if you can get some.

SERVES 6–8
TAKES 5 MINUTES, PLUS OVERNIGHT
STRAINING

500g tub Greek natural yogurt
2 tsp sesame seeds
2 tsp fresh thyme leaves,
  chopped
2 tbsp extra-virgin olive oil,
  plus extra to serve
Turkish flatbreads or pittas,
  to serve

1. Spoon the yogurt into a sieve lined with a large square of muslin. Rest over a bowl, cover with cling film and leave to drain overnight in the fridge.

2. The next day, heat a dry frying pan over a high heat. Add the sesame seeds and shake around for a few seconds until lightly toasted. Tip into a bowl, cool, then stir in the thyme and a good pinch of salt. Set aside.

3. Tip the strained yogurt into a bowl and beat with a wooden spoon until smooth. Beat in the oil and a good pinch of salt. Spoon into a small serving bowl and swirl with the back of the spoon. Drizzle with more oil and sprinkle with the sesame mix (or use zahtar).

4. Lightly toast the bread until lightly golden on both sides. Cut into fingers or wedges and serve with the yogurt dip.

★ DELICIOUS. TIP Zahtar is a blend of toasted sesame seeds, a herb similar in flavour to thyme, salt and sumac.

Coronation prawn and mango cocktail

Your guests will love this very tasty and attractive contemporary version of the classic 1970s seafood starter.

SERVES 4
READY IN 40 MINUTES

1 tbsp sunflower oil

1 small onion, finely chopped

2 tsp mild curry powder

1 tsp tomato purée

3 tbsp fresh lemon juice

3 tbsp sweet mango chutney

150ml good-quality mayonnaise

100ml Greek yogurt

1 large soft lettuce, outer leaves discarded and the rest washed and dried

1 ripe avocado, peeled, stoned and thinly sliced

1 small ripe mango, peeled, stoned and thinly sliced

300g cooked and peeled large prawns, thawed if frozen

Lightly buttered brown bread, to serve (optional)

1. Heat the sunflower oil in a small saucepan, add the onion and cook over a low heat for 5 minutes, until soft but not browned. Add the curry powder and cook for 1 minute. Add the tomato purée, 2 tablespoons of the lemon juice, the mango chutney and 150ml water, then simmer for 20–25 minutes, stirring occasionally, until reduced to a thick sauce. Transfer to a mini food processor and blend until smooth. Leave to go cold.

2. Put the mayonnaise and yogurt into a bowl with the cold curry sauce, and mix well. Season, then stir in the remaining lemon juice to taste.

3. Divide the lettuce leaves among 4 wine glasses or glass bowls and arrange the slices of avocado and mango and the prawns on top. Drizzle each with 2 tablespoons of the sauce and serve with lightly buttered brown bread, if you like.

Smoked salmon, cream cheese and watercress rolls

These are perfect party nibbles or canapés, but they also make a wonderful summertime starter.

MAKES 16
TAKES 30 MINUTES, PLUS CHILLING

4 tbsp cream cheese

2 tbsp soured cream

1 tbsp fresh lemon juice

1 tsp chopped fresh dill

16 (about 300g) smoked salmon strips, about 12cm x 3.5cm each

Bunch of fresh chives, snipped into 5cm lengths

85g watercress, stems discarded, plus extra leaves to garnish (optional)

Lemon wedges, to serve (optional)

1. In a bowl, mix together the cream cheese, soured cream and lemon juice. Season to taste, then stir in the chopped fresh dill.

2. Lay half the salmon strips on a clean work surface. Divide half the cheese mixture along the length of each, leaving a 2.5cm border at one short end. Lay some of the chives across one end of each strip, then top with some of the watercress. Roll up tightly into a neat roll, so that the chives and some watercress are sticking out. Repeat to make 16 rolls.

3. Transfer the salmon rolls to a serving plate, cover and chill until ready to serve. Garnish with extra watercress and lemon wedges, if you like.

Green gazpacho

Gazpacho is a Spanish chilled soup, usually made with tomatoes, but this version uses asparagus and cucumber for a pretty green colour.

SERVES 4

TAKES 35 MINUTES, PLUS COOLING AND CHILLING

- 500g asparagus, trimmed (or wild asparagus or hop shoots, if possible)
- 100g stale white rustic bread, diced
- 4 tbsp extra-virgin olive oil, plus extra to drizzle
- 3 tbsp sherry vinegar or wine vinegar
- 1 cucumber, peeled and seeded
- 2 garlic cloves

1. Cut the asparagus in half, separating the stalks from the tips. Bring 1 litre of water and 1 teaspoon of salt to the boil, add the tips and cook for 1½–2 minutes, until just tender. Lift out with a slotted spoon and refresh under cold water. Set aside.

2. Add the stalks to the water and simmer for 10 minutes, until very tender. Leave to cool in the liquid.

3. Pop the bread into a bowl with the oil and vinegar. Add half the cooking liquid and leave to soak for 5 minutes. Dice the cucumber and garlic and add to the bowl.

4. Put the remaining cooking liquid and stalks into a blender and blitz until smooth. Press through a sieve into a bowl and discard the pulp.

5. Put the bread mixture into the blender and whiz until smooth. Add enough of the sieved soup to get a good consistency. Season and chill.

6. Divide among bowls, drizzle with a little oil and serve garnished with the tips.

Buttered sea trout and prawn pots with dill and soda bread toast

A posh starter of citrusy seafood topped with butter and served in individual pots with crispy toast.

SERVES 6
TAKES 25 MINUTES, PLUS CHILLING

250g unsalted butter
350g skinned sea trout fillet
450g unpeeled North Atlantic prawns
1 tbsp chopped fresh dill, plus extra to garnish
Finely grated zest of ½ lemon, plus extra wedges to serve
½ tsp salt
1 loaf Irish soda bread, cut into thick slices, to serve

1. Melt 175g of the butter in a small pan. Add the trout (the butter should almost cover it) and cook over a very low heat for 8–10 minutes, carefully turning halfway.

2. Lift the trout on to a plate and leave until cool enough to handle. Set the pan of butter aside. Scrape off and discard the brown meat from the surface of the fish, and break the flesh into chunky flakes.

3. Peel the prawns. Stir the dill, lemon zest, salt, prawns and flaked sea trout into the butter left in the pan and turn over gently.

4. Spoon the mixture into 6 x 75ml tumblers or ramekins. Cover and chill for 2 hours, or until firm.

5. Melt the remaining butter. Uncover the pots and pour a thin layer over the top of each one. Return to the fridge to set.

6. Remove the pots from the fridge 15 minutes before serving. Toast the soda bread and cut into fingers. Garnish the pots with dill and serve with the toast and lemon wedges.

Variation North Atlantic prawns with their shells still on have a superior flavour, but do use ready peeled ones for ease, if you wish. You can also use salmon instead of sea trout.

Kabocha squash soup with pumpkin seed pesto

This warming soup would make a great starter for an autumnal supper party.

SERVES 4–6

TAKES 1¼–1½ HOURS, PLUS COOLING

1.25kg kabocha squash
Sunflower oil
40g butter
1 medium onion, chopped
1.2 litres vegetable stock, hot
4 tbsp crème fraîche,
  to garnish
Fresh flatleaf parsley sprigs,
  to garnish

For the pumpkin seed pesto:
30g shelled unsalted pumpkin
  seeds (from supermarkets
  and health-food shops)
40g fresh coriander leaves
½ green chilli, seeded and
  finely chopped
1 fat garlic clove, crushed
65ml olive oil
25g Parmesan, finely grated

1. Preheat the oven to 180°C/fan 160°C/gas 4. Cut the squash into chunky wedges and remove the fibres and seeds. Rub the wedges with oil, season and put into a roasting tin, skin-side down. Roast for 40 minutes. Cool, then slice away the skin and cut the flesh into small chunks.

2. Melt the butter in a large pan, add the onion and cook gently for 10 minutes until soft but not browned. Add the roasted squash and stock, then season. Cover and simmer for 20 minutes. Cool slightly.

3. Meanwhile, make the pesto. Toast the pumpkin seeds in a dry, heavy-based frying pan over a high heat. Cool, reserving 1 teaspoon for a garnish. Put the remainder into a mini food processor with the coriander, chilli, garlic and oil. Blend to a paste. Stir in the Parmesan, then season.

4. Liquidise the soup in batches until smooth. Return to the pan and bring back to a simmer. Stir in 4 tablespoons of the pesto and season to taste. Ladle into warmed bowls and garnish with the crème fraîche, reserved toasted pumpkin seeds and the flatleaf parsley.

Variation Kabocha squash is not always easy to find, so use any other variety, such as butternut or pumpkin, instead.

Buffalo mozzarella with broad bean and young leaf salad

This easy salad is unmistakably Italian. You could add some croutons or dry-cured ham, such as serrano or Parma ham.

SERVES 4
READY IN 20 MINUTES

300g podded fresh or frozen broad beans

100g young salad leaves (we used wild garlic leaves, pea shoots and cress) or rocket

500g buffalo mozzarella or feta, broken into rough, bite-sized pieces

For the dressing:

2 garlic cloves, crushed

Juice of 1 lemon

5 tbsp cold-pressed rapeseed oil or olive oil

A little chopped fresh mint

1. Cook the beans in plenty of salted boiling water for no more than 2 minutes, until just tender. Drain and refresh under cold water. Squeeze the beans gently with your thumb and forefinger to remove the tough skins (you don't have to, but they will look spectacular and are easier to digest). Set aside.

2. Make the dressing. Mix together the garlic, lemon juice, rapeseed or olive oil, mint and some salt.

3. Arrange the salad leaves, beans and cheese on plates, and serve with the dressing drizzled over.

Pea, lettuce and tarragon soup

This refreshing soup uses plenty of greens to give it a vibrant colour and memorable flavour.

SERVES 4
READY IN 25 MINUTES

40g butter

6 spring onions, trimmed and sliced

675g freshly shelled or frozen peas

Leaves from 4 fresh tarragon sprigs

225g romaine lettuce, finely shredded

1 litre fresh vegetable stock, hot

2 tbsp crème fraîche

Watercress sprigs, to garnish (optional)

Crusty fresh bread, to serve

1. Melt the butter in a large saucepan over a medium heat. Add the spring onions and cook, stirring, for 2 minutes. Stir in three-quarters of the peas, half the tarragon and all the lettuce. Cook for 1 minute. Add the stock, bring to the boil, cover and simmer for 8–10 minutes, if the peas are fresh, 5 minutes if frozen, or until they are tender.

2. Whiz the soup in a blender with the remaining tarragon, until smooth. Pass through a fine sieve into a clean saucepan. Stir in the rest of the peas and simmer gently for 4–5 minutes or until the peas are just tender. Season to taste.

3. Divide the soup among bowls, swirl the crème fraîche into each serving and garnish with watercress sprigs, if you like. Serve with some crusty fresh bread.

Variation This soup would also be wonderful made with fresh mint leaves instead of tarragon.

Baked mussels with chilli, anchovy and caper breadcrumbs

Mussels have never been nicer than in this easy recipe – here they're mixed with chilli, anchovies and capers.

MAKES ABOUT 50 (SERVES 10)
READY IN 30 MINUTES

3 tbsp olive oil

4 shallots, very finely chopped

1 medium–hot red chilli, seeded and very finely chopped

Pinch of crushed dried chillies

2 anchovy fillets in olive oil (from a can), drained and chopped

50g white breadcrumbs, made from stale bread

1 tbsp capers, drained, rinsed and chopped

1½ tbsp chopped fresh flatleaf parsley

1kg mussels, scrubbed and beards removed

50ml dry white wine

Juice of ½ small lemon

1. Heat the oil in a frying pan over a medium heat. Add the shallots, red chilli and dried chillies, and cook for 5 minutes, until soft but not browned. Add the anchovies and stir until they have melted. Lower the heat, add the breadcrumbs and stir for 2–3 minutes until lightly browned. Stir in the capers, parsley and seasoning. Set aside.

2. Preheat the oven to 220°C/fan 200°C/gas 7. Discard any mussels that are cracked or that don't close when given a tap on the work surface.

3. Heat a large pan over a high heat. Add the mussels and wine, cover and shake over a high heat for 2–3 minutes until they have just opened. Drain and leave to cool slightly. Discard any mussels that remain closed. Break off and discard the empty half-shell from the remainder and lay them side by side on a baking sheet.

4. Spoon a little of the breadcrumb mix on top of each mussel. Drizzle with 2–3 drops of lemon juice. Bake for 3 minutes, until lightly golden. Serve immediately.

Seared scallops on pea and mint risotto

This fresh and flavourful first course is bound to impress.

SERVES 6
READY IN 35 MINUTES

15g unsalted butter
1 tbsp olive oil
300g roeless small (queen) scallops, thawed if frozen
Fresh baby mint leaves, to serve

For the pea and mint risotto:
1.2 litres chicken or vegetable stock, hot
75g butter
8 spring onions, trimmed and finely chopped
225g risotto rice
50ml dry white vermouth or white wine
225g freshly shelled or frozen peas
2 tbsp chopped fresh mint
25g Parmesan, finely grated

1. Make the risotto. Pour the stock into a pan and keep hot over a low heat. Melt 50g of butter in another pan, add the spring onions and cook for 1 minute. Stir in the rice, then the vermouth or wine and simmer, stirring, for 1 minute. Add a ladleful of stock and simmer, stirring, until it has been absorbed before adding another. Continue like this for 20–25 minutes until the rice is tender but still al dente.

2. Meanwhile, cook the peas in boiling salted water for 4–5 minutes. Drain well, put into a food processor with the remaining butter and the mint, and process until smooth. Set aside.

3. When the risotto has 4 minutes to go, heat a large, non-stick frying pan over a high heat. Reduce the heat slightly, add the butter, oil and half the scallops, and sear for 1 minute on each side, seasoning them as they cook. Spoon on to a plate and keep warm while you cook the remainder.

4. Stir the pea purée into the risotto with the Parmesan and some seasoning. Spoon on to warmed serving plates and pile the scallops on top. Scatter with the mint leaves and serve.

comfort food

Crispy crackling stuffed roast pork with roasted apples

Family and friends will love this traditional roast, served with roasted apples instead of the usual apple sauce.

SERVES 6
READY IN 2 HOURS 20 MINUTES

1.5kg boned-out spare rib of pork
1 heaped tbsp chopped fresh sage
Finely grated zest of ½ lemon
Sunflower oil, for greasing the tin
4 firm eating apples, such as Cox's or Braeburns
50g butter, melted
1 tsp plain flour
600ml light stock, made from pork or chicken bones

For the stuffing:
1 medium onion, finely chopped
25g butter, plus extra to brush the top of the stuffing
100g fresh white breadcrumbs
Finely grated zest of ½ lemon
1 heaped tbsp chopped fresh sage
1 tbsp chopped fresh curly parsley
½ beaten egg

1. Preheat the oven to 240°C/fan 220°C/gas 9. Unroll the pork and score the skin. Sprinkle the meat with the sage, lemon zest and seasoning. Reshape the joint and tie with string. Salt the skin, put in an oiled roasting tin, skin-side up, and roast for 20 minutes. Reduce the oven to 180°C/fan 160°C/gas 4 and roast for 25 minutes per 450g.

2. Meanwhile, for the stuffing, fry the onion in the butter until lightly browned. Mix with the breadcrumbs, lemon zest, sage, parsley, seasoning and egg. Spoon into a shallow ovenproof dish.

3. About 30 minutes before the pork is ready, peel, core and quarter the apples. Toss them with the melted butter, spoon around the pork and return to the oven. Brush the stuffing with the remaining butter and roast alongside the pork.

4. Remove the pork from the oven and rest for 10 minutes. Turn off the oven and keep the apples and stuffing hot.

5. Pour the fat out of the tin, then put it over a medium heat. Stir in the flour and then the stock, and simmer until reduced. Carve the pork and serve with the gravy, apples and stuffing.

Creamy chicken, chive and mustard gratin

A comforting winter dish with a creamy filling and crunchy, oozy topping.

SERVES 2
TAKES 15 MINUTES, PLUS
20 MINUTES IN THE OVEN

300g floury potatoes, thinly sliced
25g butter
25g plain flour
600ml chicken stock
100ml half-fat crème fraîche
1 tbsp Dijon mustard
Approx. 350g cooked shredded chicken
Bunch of fresh chives, snipped, plus 2 tbsp extra to garnish
40g Cheshire or Caerphilly cheese, crumbled
40g fresh breadcrumbs

1. Preheat the oven to 200°C/fan 180°C/ gas 6. Bring a saucepan of water to the boil, add the potatoes and cook for 6–8 minutes, until nearly cooked through. Drain well.

2. Make the sauce. Melt the butter in a saucepan, stir in the flour and cook for 2 minutes, until it forms a smooth paste. Add the stock, a little at a time, and simmer, stirring continuously, until you have a smooth, thickened sauce.

3. Stir the crème fraîche and mustard into the sauce, and heat for a few minutes. Add the chicken and chives, and season to taste.

4. Spoon the mixture into a 1.5-litre gratin or ovenproof baking dish and arrange the potatoes on top. Sprinkle over the cheese and breadcrumbs, and bake for 20 minutes, until the top is pale golden and the filling bubbling hot. Preheat the grill to High and grill the gratin for 5 minutes to crisp up the topping. Scatter with the extra chives and serve.

Fish pie with prawns and cheesy leek mash topping

This satisfying fish pie has a moreish cheesy topping, making it the perfect comfort food.

SERVES 6
READY IN 1 HOUR

600ml milk

300ml whipping cream

450g white fish fillet, such as cod, haddock or coley

225g smoked haddock or smoked cod fillet

175g cooked and peeled small prawns, thawed if frozen

3 hard-boiled eggs, peeled and roughly chopped

100g butter

45g plain flour

3 tbsp chopped fresh parsley

1kg peeled floury potatoes, such as Maris Piper, cut into large chunks

1 large leek, thinly sliced and washed well

75g Cheddar, coarsely grated

1. Bring 450ml of the milk and the cream to the boil in a large pan. Add the fish and simmer for 5–6 minutes. Lift on to a plate to cool. Strain the liquid into a jug.

2. Flake the fish into a 1.75-litre shallow ovenproof dish, discarding the skin and bones. Scatter over the prawns and eggs.

3. Melt 50g of the butter in a pan, add the flour and cook, stirring, for 1 minute. Gradually stir in the reserved cooking liquid, bring to the boil, then simmer for 5 minutes, stirring. Stir in the parsley, season and pour over the fish. Leave to go cold.

4. Preheat the oven to 200°C/fan 180°C/gas 6. Cook the potatoes in boiling salted water for 20 minutes. Meanwhile, cook the leek gently in the remaining butter for 3–4 minutes, until tender.

5. Drain the potatoes, return to the pan and mash until smooth. Stir in the leek, cheese and a little milk to make a spreadable mash. Season.

6. Spoon the mash evenly over the pie and bake for 35–40 minutes, until bubbling and golden brown.

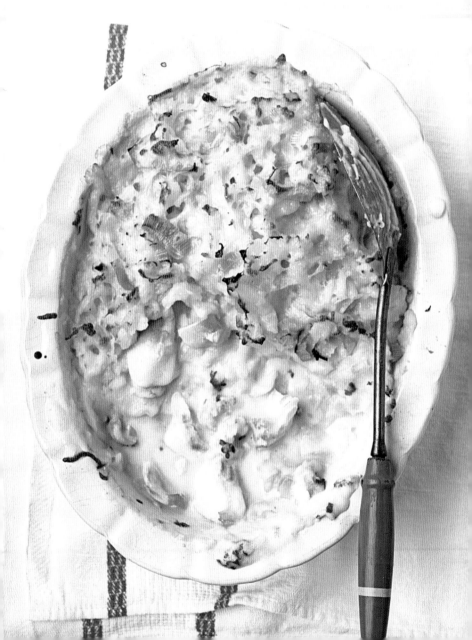

Braised lamb shanks

These lamb shanks are deceptively easy to cook and yet smart enough to serve at a dinner party for friends.

SERVES 6
TAKES 30 MINUTES, PLUS 1½ HOURS IN THE OVEN

2 carrots, finely diced
2 celery sticks, finely diced
3–4 tbsp olive oil
Few fresh thyme sprigs
3 bay leaves
3 garlic cloves, finely chopped
3 tbsp concentrated tomato purée
¾ bottle white wine
375ml lamb stock (or water)
6 lamb shanks
Fresh parsley, chopped

1. Preheat the oven to 150°C/fan 130°C/gas 2. In a flameproof casserole dish, fry the vegetables in some of the olive oil, without browning, until tender. Add the thyme, bay leaves, garlic, tomato purée, wine and stock or water. Bring to the boil and lower to a gentle simmer.

2. Heat a little more olive oil in a separate pan and brown the shanks on all sides, seasoning as you go. Transfer to the casserole dish, cover, and cook in the oven for 1½ hours, until the meat is tender and coming off the bone.

3. Remove the shanks from the pan and keep warm while you finish the sauce. Skim off some of the fat that is floating on the surface. Boil to reduce and concentrate the flavour, if you think it needs it. Taste for seasoning. Serve a lamb shank on each warmed plate with some sauce spooned over, together with some Mediterranean vegetables.

Moussaka

This classic recipe includes a hint of cinnamon and is topped with a lovely mixture of yogurt and cheese, which browns and bubbles up attractively during cooking.

SERVES 4
TAKES 50 MINUTES, PLUS
35 MINUTES IN THE OVEN

1 tbsp olive oil, plus extra for brushing
1 large onion, finely chopped
2 garlic cloves, crushed
500g minced lamb
1 tbsp tomato purée
½ tsp ground cinnamon
400g can chopped tomatoes
2 tsp dried oregano
600g (about 2 medium) aubergines

For the topping:
150ml Greek yogurt
1 medium egg, beaten
25g freshly grated Parmesan
50g feta

1. Heat the oil in a large frying pan over a medium heat. Add the onion and garlic, and cook, stirring, for 5 minutes, until soft. Increase the heat, add the minced lamb and cook for 5 minutes, until browned.

2. Add the purée and cinnamon, and simmer for 1 minute. Add the tomatoes, then half-fill the can with water and pour into the pan. Add the oregano, season, and simmer, stirring occasionally, for 20 minutes.

3. Meanwhile, preheat the grill to Medium–High. Cut each aubergine diagonally into 5mm-thick slices. Brush with oil and grill for 2½ minutes on each side, in batches if necessary, until golden. Drain on kitchen paper.

4. Preheat the oven to 200°C/fan 180°C/gas 6. For the topping, mix the yogurt, egg and half the cheeses. Season with pepper.

5. Spread half the lamb mixture in a deep, 1.2-litre ovenproof dish and cover with half the aubergines. Repeat, then spoon over the yogurt mixture and scatter with the remaining cheeses. Bake for 35 minutes, until golden and bubbling.

Roots, ham and caramelised onion pie

Everyone loves a nice pastry-topped pie, and this one will be no exception.

SERVES 6

TAKES 45 MINUTES, PLUS
40 MINUTES IN THE OVEN

90g butter

12 whole pickling onions or small shallots, peeled and halved

1 fresh thyme sprig, leaves picked

2 tsp caster sugar

225g carrots, cut into small chunks

225g swede, cut into chunks

225g celeriac, cut into chunks

30g plain flour, plus extra for dusting

600ml full-fat milk

50g fresh Parmesan, grated

Good handful of chopped fresh parsley

225g piece cooked ham, cut into chunks

375g ready-rolled shortcrust pastry

1 medium egg, beaten

1. Melt 50g of the butter in a large pan over a low heat, add the onions, cover and cook for 15–20 minutes, stirring occasionally, until tender. Increase the heat slightly, add the thyme and sugar and cook, uncovered, for 5–6 minutes, until caramelised. Cool.

2. Meanwhile, steam the rest of the vegetables for 10–12 minutes, until tender. Drain well.

3. Preheat the oven to 200°C/fan 180°C/gas 6. Make the sauce. Melt the remaining butter in a pan, add the flour and cook, stirring, for 1 minute. Gradually stir in the milk, bring to the boil, then simmer for 2 minutes, stirring. Remove from the heat and stir in the cheese, parsley, vegetables, ham and onions. Season, then spoon into a 2-litre pie dish. Cover the dish with the pastry, trim the edges and use the trimmings to decorate the pie, if you wish.

4. Brush the pastry with the egg, cut a small cross in the centre and sit it on a baking sheet. Bake for 40 minutes, until golden.

Variation Replace the cooked ham with some cooked, flaked chicken if you wish, or use a mix of the two.

Fragrant chicken stew

The saffron and fennel in this wonderful stew give it a mildly exotic flavour.

SERVES 4
TAKES ABOUT 1 HOUR

Good pinch of saffron strands
3 tbsp olive oil
1.5–1.75kg chicken, jointed into 8 pieces
12–16 shallots
2 fennel bulbs, sliced
125g pancetta or bacon lardons
2 garlic cloves, finely chopped
1 tsp fennel seeds, lightly crushed
1 tbsp Pernod (optional)
250ml dry white wine
350ml chicken stock, hot
3 fresh thyme sprigs, leaves picked
2 fresh bay leaves
2 tbsp butter, softened
2 tbsp plain flour
4 tbsp crème fraîche
2 tbsp chopped fresh parsley, to serve

1. Soak the saffron in 1 tablespoon of hot water. Heat the oil in a large flameproof casserole dish. Season the chicken pieces, add to the oil and brown. Set aside. Add the shallots and fry until golden. Set aside. Add the fennel and fry until golden. Set aside.

2. Pour away all but 1 teaspoon of oil from the casserole, add the pancetta or lardons and fry until golden. Add the garlic and fennel seeds, and fry for a few seconds. Add the Pernod, if you like, and wine, bubble briefly, then add the stock, herbs and saffron water.

3. Return the chicken and shallots to the casserole dish, cover and simmer for 5 minutes. Stir in the fennel, cover and simmer for 35 minutes, or until the chicken is tender.

4. Mix the butter and flour together into a smooth paste. Stir into the stew, a little at a time, until the sauce has thickened. Simmer for 2–3 minutes. Stir in the crème fraîche and season. Scatter with the parsley and serve.

Variation For a more down-to-earth version of this stew, replace the saffron and fennel with celery and carrots.

Roasted Mediterranean vegetable lasagne

If you're cooking for vegetarians, nothing could be nicer than this dish. Serve it with a crisp salad and hot garlic bread.

SERVES 6–8
READY IN 1½ HOURS

2 small aubergines, cut into 2.5cm chunks
2 red onions, cut into wedges
2 red peppers, seeded and cut into chunky strips
4 garlic cloves, finely chopped
5 tbsp olive oil
450g courgettes, sliced
225g fresh lasagne sheets
50g Parmesan, finely grated

For the sauce:
60g butter
70g plain flour
900ml milk
125g Cheddar, coarsely grated

1. Preheat the oven to 220°C/fan 200°C/gas 7. In a large roasting tin, toss the aubergines, onions, peppers and garlic with 3 tablespoons of oil. Season, then roast for 30 minutes, or until soft.

2. Meanwhile, fry the courgettes in the remaining oil until browned. Remove the vegetables from the oven and stir in the courgettes. Lower the oven to 200°C/fan 180°C/gas 6.

3. Make the sauce. Melt the butter in a pan, stir in the flour and cook for 1 minute. Gradually stir in the milk. Bring to the boil, stirring, then simmer gently for 10 minutes, stirring occasionally.

4. Cook the lasagne according to the packet instructions. Drain and dry on a clean tea towel.

5. Add the cheese to the sauce and season. Spoon a thin layer over the base of a shallow 2.4-litre ovenproof dish. Cover with 4 lasagne sheets. Top with half the vegetables, then one-third of the remaining sauce and another 4 sheets of lasagne. Repeat once more. Spread over the remaining sauce and sprinkle with Parmesan. Bake for 40 minutes, until golden and bubbling.

Indonesian beef rendang

This is a delicious, mild beef curry from the Far East, flavoured with coconut milk and lemongrass.

SERVES 4–6
READY IN 3 HOURS

2 lemongrass stalks, outer layer removed and reserved

2 large red chillies, seeded and chopped

6 garlic cloves, roughly chopped

5cm piece fresh root ginger, roughly chopped

1 large onion, roughly chopped

½ tsp ground ginger

1 tbsp ground coriander

1 tsp ground cumin

1 tsp freshly ground black pepper

2 tbsp sunflower oil

2 cinnamon sticks

12 cloves

2 bay leaves

600ml canned coconut milk

1.5kg braising steak, such as chuck or blade, cut into 5cm pieces

1 tsp salt

Walnut-sized piece of tamarind pulp or 2 tbsp lemon juice

1 tbsp dark muscovado sugar

Plain rice and a cucumber, tomato, red onion and coriander salsa, to serve

1. Chop the lemongrass core and put into a mini food processor with the chillies, garlic, fresh ginger, onion, ground ginger, coriander, cumin, black pepper and 2 tablespoons of water. Blend to a smooth paste.

2. Heat the oil in a large flameproof casserole dish over a medium heat. Add the cinnamon and cloves, and sizzle for 1 minute. Add the spice paste and bay leaves, and fry for 2 minutes. Add the coconut milk, 200ml water, the beef, reserved lemongrass leaves and salt, and bring to the boil.

3. Meanwhile, if you are using tamarind, put it into a small bowl with 120ml of warm water and mash with your fingers to release the seeds. Strain into a clean bowl and discard the seeds.

4. Lower the heat to a simmer, add the tamarind liquid or lemon juice and sugar, and simmer, uncovered, for 2½ hours, stirring more frequently as the liquid reduces, until the sauce is quite thick and the beef very tender. Serve with plain rice and a cucumber, tomato, red onion and coriander salsa.

Normandy pork with cider

The Dijon mustard and crème fraîche give this French recipe a lovely creamy flavour that complements the pork perfectly.

SERVES 8

TAKES 1¾ HOURS

4 tbsp vegetable oil

1kg lean pork, diced

2 large onions, diced

2 large carrots, thickly sliced

2 parsnips, thickly sliced

2 leeks, washed and sliced into 3cm lengths

500ml dry cider

2 bay leaves

1 tsp Dijon mustard

1 tbsp cornflour

200g half-fat crème fraîche

2 Cox's apples

1. Heat the oil in a large frying pan over a medium–high heat. Fry the pork in batches, until just browned. Remove with a slotted spoon and put in a casserole dish.

2. Add the onions to the frying pan and fry for 5 minutes, stirring. Add to the pork with the vegetables, pour over the cider and add the bay leaves. Bring to the boil, cover and simmer for 1 hour, or until the pork is tender. Cool slightly.

3. Stir the mustard and cornflour into the crème fraîche. Quarter the apples, core and cut into wedges. Stir the apples into the casserole with the crème-fraîche mixture and simmer for 5–8 minutes, until the apples are tender and the sauce has thickened. Season and serve.

Maple syrup and mustard gammon with creamy gratin

The slightly salty gammon is sweetened with a touch of maple syrup and given a kick with wholegrain mustard.

SERVES 4

TAKES 10 MINUTES, PLUS 1 HOUR 20 MINUTES IN THE OVEN, PLUS STANDING

1kg smoked gammon joint
2 tbsp maple syrup or runny honey
1 tbsp wholegrain mustard
1 tsp coarsely crushed black peppercorns
Green vegetables, to serve

For the creamy gratin:
1kg potatoes, thinly sliced
1 onion, finely chopped
25g butter
50g plain flour
750ml semi-skimmed milk

1. Preheat the oven to 200°C/fan 180°C/gas 6. Make the creamy gratin. Put a quarter of the potatoes in a casserole dish, sprinkle with a third of the onion, dot with a third of the butter, then sprinkle with a third of the flour. Season well. Repeat, then finish with a final layer of potato. Pour over the milk and cook for 1 hour 20 minutes, until the potatoes are tender and golden and the sauce has thickened. Put the gammon into a small roasting tin. Cover with foil and cook above the potatoes for 1 hour.

2. Meanwhile, mix together the maple syrup, mustard and peppercorns. After 1 hour, remove the gammon from the oven and slice away the skin, leaving the layer of fat behind. Score the fat in a diamond pattern and spread over the maple-syrup mixture. Return to the oven, uncovered, for a further 20 minutes.

3. Leave the gammon and gratin to stand for 5 minutes. Then carve the gammon into slices and serve with the gratin and some green vegetables.

★ DELICIOUS. TIP Soak the gammon overnight in plenty of cold water to reduce the saltiness before cooking, if you like.

Oven-baked porcini mushroom and taleggio rice

This rich and creamy rice dish would make the perfect hearty lunch, served with a very simple mixed leaf salad.

SERVES 4

TAKES 45 MINUTES, PLUS 35 MINUTES IN THE OVEN, PLUS SOAKING

20g dried porcini mushrooms
200g chestnut mushrooms
150g small field mushrooms
90g butter
1 large onion, finely chopped
4 fresh thyme sprigs, leaves picked
250g risotto rice, such as arborio
Good splash of dry white wine
225ml chicken or vegetable stock, hot, plus extra if necessary
Grated fresh nutmeg, to taste
3 tbsp finely grated Parmesan
200g taleggio cheese
Mixed leaf salad, to serve

1. Cover the porcini mushrooms with 900ml boiling water and soak for 30 minutes. Roughly chop the fresh mushrooms into 2.5cm pieces.

2. Melt the butter in a 3-litre flameproof casserole dish. Add the onion and cook gently for 7–8 minutes until soft but not browned.

3. Drain the porcini, reserving the liquid. Cut them into thin strips and add to the onions with the fresh mushrooms and thyme leaves. Cook for 15 minutes, stirring occasionally.

4. Meanwhile, preheat the oven to 150°C/fan 130°C/gas 2. Stir the rice into the mushrooms with the wine, mushroom liquor, stock and grated nutmeg. Season and bring up to a simmer. Transfer to the oven and cook, uncovered, for 20 minutes.

5. Give the rice a good stir, then stir in the Parmesan. Return to the oven for a further 15 minutes.

6. Meanwhile, preheat the grill to High. Cut the taleggio into very thin slices. Remove the rice from the oven, season and stir in a little stock, if necessary, to give it a creamy texture. Lay the taleggio over the top and grill for 1–2 minutes.

Braised beef and winter vegetable stew

Pickled or even braised red cabbage would make a fantastic accompaniment to this tasty beef stew.

SERVES 4

TAKES 30 MINUTES, PLUS 2½ HOURS ON THE HOB

2 tbsp olive oil

1.6kg piece rolled and tied brisket, blade or braising steak

2 carrots, halved lengthways and cut into large chunks

2 celery sticks, chopped

2 onions, cut into small wedges

400g can chopped tomatoes

2 bay leaves

1 litre hot beef stock, made from 1 stock cube

250g dried country vegetable mixture, including split peas, lentils and pearl barley

Small handful of fresh flatleaf parsley, finely chopped

1. Heat the oil in a large flameproof casserole dish and sear the beef all over until just browned. Add all of the fresh vegetables and bay leaves to the casserole with the stock. Bring to the boil, then cover, reduce the heat and simmer gently for 1 hour.

2. Stir the split peas, lentils and pearl barley into the stew and continue to cook for a further 1½ hours, until the stock is thickened and the pulses are cooked and tender.

3. Lift the beef on to a board and cut into thick slices, discarding the string. Ladle the stewed vegetables and pulses into bowls and serve with the beef slices and a good sprinkling of chopped parsley.

Variation Vegetarians can omit the beef and cook the split peas, lentils, pearl barley and vegetables in vegetable stock. They are wonderful served with a nut roast.

al fresco
fare

Seared tuna with tomato and caper salsa and pesto beans

This Italian tuna recipe is full of the flavours of the Mediterranean: tomatoes, garlic, chilli, capers and basil.

SERVES 4
READY IN 20 MINUTES

4 x 200g tuna steaks, cut about 3cm thick
Olive oil, for brushing

For the salsa:
2 large vine-ripened tomatoes, skinned and roughly chopped
1 large shallot, halved and thinly sliced into fine wedges
1 garlic clove, thinly sliced
1 green chilli, seeded and finely chopped
Pinch of crushed dried chillies
1 tbsp small capers, drained and rinsed
Juice of 1 lime
1 tbsp olive oil
1 tbsp each chopped fresh mint and flatleaf parsley

For the pesto green beans:
40g fresh basil leaves
25g pine nuts
1 garlic clove, crushed
5 tbsp olive oil
25g finely grated Parmesan
500g fine green beans

1. Make the salsa. Mix the tomatoes, shallot, garlic, chillies, capers, lime juice and oil together in a bowl and set aside.

2. Make the pesto beans. Bring a pan of salted water to the boil. Meanwhile, whiz the basil, pine nuts, garlic and oil to a paste in a mini food processor. Stir in the Parmesan. Cook the beans in the boiling water for 4–5 minutes, or until tender. Drain, return to the pan with half the pesto and mix well.

3. Brush the tuna with oil, then season. Heat a cast-iron griddle over a high heat. Add the tuna, reduce the heat, and cook for 1½ minutes on each side, until nicely marked on the outside but still quite rare in the centre.

4. Transfer the tuna to plates. Add the mint, parsley and a little salt to the salsa. Serve the tuna steaks with the salsa and pesto green beans.

★ DELICIOUS. TIP The leftover pesto will keep, covered, in the fridge for up to 2 days; you can freeze it in an ice-cube tray for later use.

Roll-your-own chilli steak fajitas

This dish is ideal for feeding a large crowd. You simply put everything into the centre of the table and let everyone help themselves.

SERVES 6

TAKES 25 MINUTES, PLUS MARINATING

3 tbsp olive oil

2 garlic cloves, crushed

1 tsp chilli powder

2 tsp ground coriander

1 tsp ground cumin

1kg sirloin steak, cut into strips

12–18 soft flour tortillas

2 red peppers, seeded and cut into strips

2 yellow peppers, seeded and cut into strips

3 large field mushrooms, sliced

2 handfuls of fresh coriander leaves, to serve

Soured cream, grated cheese, tomato salsa and guacamole, to serve

1. Mix 2 tablespoons of the oil, the garlic, chilli powder, ground coriander, ground cumin and some seasoning together in a glass bowl. Stir in the steak, cover and marinate in the fridge for about 3 hours.

2. When you are ready to eat, wrap the tortillas in foil and place them in an oven on a low heat to heat through.

3. Heat a large cast-iron griddle pan until very hot. Toss the peppers and mushrooms in the remaining oil, throw them on the griddle pan, and cook, tossing occasionally, for 3–4 minutes until tender. Transfer to a plate and keep warm in the oven.

4. Re-heat the pan, add the steak and its marinade and toss for another 3–4 minutes until just cooked through. Return the peppers and mushrooms to the pan and toss together to mix.

5. Take the pan to the table, along with the warm tortillas, fresh coriander, soured cream, cheese, tomato salsa and guacamole.

Variation You could also make these fajitas with chicken instead. Just cut skinless chicken breasts into thin strips, and griddle until cooked through.

Pork and chorizo kebabs

The bread in these kebabs soaks up all the lovely spices and juices that come from the chorizo – which in turn prevents the bread burning.

MAKES 6
TAKES 20 MINUTES, PLUS
10–12 MINUTES ON THE BARBECUE,
PLUS 30 MINUTES SOAKING

2 pork tenderloins, each about 350–450g
2 thick slices Granary bread
200g thin piece chorizo, cut into 24 slices
6 tbsp olive oil
½ tsp paprika
1 tbsp chopped fresh sage
Vegetable oil, for brushing
Couscous, grilled tomatoes and rocket, to serve

1. Light your barbecue. If you are using wooden or bamboo skewers, soak 6 of them in cold water for at least 30 minutes before using.

2. Meanwhile, trim the pork of any excess fat, then cut into 24 bite-sized cubes. Cut the bread into 24 cubes, slightly smaller than the pork. Thread 4 pork pieces, 4 bread pieces and 4 chorizo slices alternately on to each skewer.

3. Mix the olive oil with the paprika, sage and some seasoning, and brush over the skewers, making sure you soak the bread well.

4. Brush the cooking grate with a little vegetable oil. Barbecue the skewers directly over a medium heat for 10–12 minutes – turning halfway and brushing with any remaining paprika oil – until cooked through. Serve with some couscous, grilled tomatoes and rocket.

★ DELICIOUS. TIP If you prefer, cook these kebabs under a medium–hot grill for 15 minutes, turning once. But if you do, omit the bread.

Variation Chorizo also has a great affinity with chicken, so you could replace the pork with cubes of skinless chicken breast, if you wish.

Sweet and sour prawns with lime

This is a quick recipe that can be thrown on to a summer barbecue for a satisfying and succulent flavour of the Far East.

MAKES 4
TAKES 10 MINUTES, 2–3 MINUTES ON THE BARBECUE, PLUS MARINATING AND 30 MINUTES SOAKING

16 large raw prawns, peeled and deveined
2 tbsp olive oil
1 garlic clove, crushed
2 tbsp light soy sauce
1–2 tbsp clear honey
2 limes
2 tbsp roughly chopped fresh coriander
Pinch of chilli flakes
Tomato salad, to serve

1. Light your barbecue. Soak 4 bamboo or wooden skewers in cold water for at least 30 minutes.

2. Meanwhile, rinse the prawns and pat dry on kitchen paper. Put into a bowl and set aside. Mix together the olive oil, garlic, soy sauce, honey, the zest and juice of 1 lime, coriander, chilli and seasoning. Pour it over the prawns and toss well. Cover and marinate in the fridge for 15 minutes.

3. Cut the other lime into quarters. Thread 4 prawns and 1 lime wedge on to each skewer. Barbecue the prawns directly over a medium heat for 2–3 minutes, turning halfway, and brushing with any remaining marinade, until pink and tender. Serve with a tomato salad.

★ DELICIOUS. TIP You could also cook these under a medium–hot grill for 8–10 minutes, turning once.

Barbecued leg of lamb with tomato and mint salsa

The red wine, garlic and herbs in the marinade pack the meat with flavour and tenderise it to make cooking quicker.

SERVES 6
TAKES 40–50 MINUTES, PLUS
OVERNIGHT MARINATING

1.3–1.5kg leg of lamb, boned and butterflied
3 garlic cloves, sliced
3 shallots, halved
Few fresh rosemary sprigs
3 bay leaves
Few fresh oregano sprigs
375ml red wine
Vegetable oil, for brushing

For the tomato and mint salsa:
6 ripe plum or vine tomatoes
Small bunch of fresh mint, leaves picked
Good pinch of caster sugar
Bunch of spring onions, thinly sliced
2 garlic cloves, crushed
1 tbsp extra-virgin olive oil
2 tsp balsamic vinegar

1. Put the lamb into a large freezer bag with the garlic, shallots and herbs. Carefully pour in the wine, then seal and put into a container in the fridge. Leave to marinate for 24 hours – or 48 hours for a more intense flavour.

2. A few hours before you want to eat, make the salsa. Cut the tomatoes in half, scoop out the seeds and discard. Dice the flesh and put into a bowl. Chop the mint leaves and add to the tomatoes with the sugar, onions, garlic, olive oil and balsamic vinegar. Stir well, then set aside.

3. Light your barbecue. Take the lamb out of the marinade and discard the marinade. Brush the cooking grate with oil. Barbecue the lamb over a direct medium heat for 20–30 minutes, turning once. This will give you medium-cooked meat. If you like your lamb rare, reduce the cooking time by about 5 minutes. Leave to rest for 5 minutes before slicing. Serve with the salsa.

★ DELICIOUS. TIP A butterflied leg of lamb has had the bones removed and the meat opened up so that it is all of similar thickness. Get the butcher to do this, as it can be quite time-consuming.

Best-ever tandoori chicken

This barbecue recipe is one of those dishes you will want to make every summer, rain or shine.

SERVES 6
TAKES 15 MINUTES, PLUS
15–18 MINUTES ON THE BARBECUE,
PLUS 1–6 HOURS MARINATING

4 free-range chicken legs
4 boneless skinless
  free-range chicken thighs
3 boneless skinless free-range
  chicken breasts, cut into large
  pieces
Juice of ½ lemon
1 tbsp paprika
6 garlic cloves, crushed
7.5cm piece fresh ginger, sliced
3 tbsp sunflower oil, plus extra
  for brushing
1½ tsp cardamom seeds, finely
  ground
2 tbsp garam masala
250ml wholemilk natural
  yogurt
40g unsalted butter, melted
Mint raita, warm coriander
  naan bread and lemon
  wedges, to serve

1. Slash both sides of each leg and thigh, and put into a bowl with the breast pieces. Sprinkle with the lemon juice, paprika and some salt, and mix well. Cover and set aside for 30 minutes.

2. Put the garlic, ginger, oil, cardamom, garam masala and yogurt into a liquidiser, and blend thoroughly. Add to the chicken and mix well. Cover and chill for 1–6 hours.

3. Light your barbecue. Shake the excess marinade off the chicken and thread the breast pieces and thighs on to long skewers. Brush the chicken and the bars of the grate with oil.

4. Cook the chicken directly over a high heat for 4 minutes each side, releasing with a wide spatula and turning now and then until nicely marked by the grate. Then remove to a plate and brush with melted butter.

5. Turn off the middle burner or push the coals to either side of the grate. Return the chicken to the grate and continue to cook over an indirect high heat for 3–5 minutes each side, until cooked through. Serve with raita, naan bread and lemon wedges.

★ DELICIOUS. TIP You can also cook the chicken in the oven, set to its highest temperature, on a rack set in a roasting tin for about 20 minutes, until cooked through.

Crispy cos, anchovy, egg and crouton salad with a creamy cheese dressing

A simple, quick salad with a wonderful Parmesan dressing.

SERVES 8
READY IN 20 MINUTES

8 ciabatta slices
2 tbsp olive oil, plus extra for greasing
4 medium eggs
2 cos or romaine lettuce hearts, outer leaves discarded
75g fresh (from supermarket deli counters) or canned anchovy fillets in olive oil, drained
Small block Parmesan or Grana Padano, for shaving

For the dressing:
1 small garlic clove, crushed
1 large very fresh egg yolk
1 tsp Dijon mustard
2 tbsp fresh lemon juice
4 tbsp finely grated Parmesan or Grana Padano
150ml extra-virgin olive oil
2 tbsp double cream

1. Preheat the oven to 180°C/fan 160°C/gas 4. Tear the ciabatta into small pieces and toss in a bowl with the olive oil. Place on a baking sheet and bake for 5–7 minutes, until crisp and golden. Leave to cool, then season lightly with salt.

2. Meanwhile, cook the eggs in a pan of boiling water for 7 minutes. Drain and cover with cold water.

3. Make the dressing. Put the garlic, egg yolk, mustard, lemon juice, Parmesan and some seasoning into a small bowl. Mix together with an electric hand whisk, then slowly whisk in the oil to make a smooth dressing. Stir in the cream. Chill until needed.

4. Tear the lettuce into small pieces and toss with 4 tablespoons of the dressing. Divide among 8 serving plates or bowls.

5. Peel the eggs and cut into quarters. Arrange over the lettuce leaves with the anchovy fillets and croutons. Drizzle over the remaining dressing. Shave over the cheese and serve.

Note: This recipe contains raw egg.

Variation To make this into a more substantial main course, serve it with some griddled mini chicken fillets that have been marinated in fresh lemon juice and olive oil.

Feta and slow-roasted tomato salad

Giving the tomatoes a long, gentle roast in the oven helps to bring out their flavour – absolutely heavenly!

SERVES 4
TAKES 20 MINUTES, PLUS
1½–1¾ HOURS IN THE OVEN

8 plum tomatoes, halved lengthways
2 tbsp olive oil
200g baby courgettes, halved lengthways, or small courgettes, sliced on the diagonal
½ cucumber, diced
1 small red onion, thinly sliced
130g jar mixed pitted Greek olives in oil, drained
1 romaine lettuce, torn into pieces
200g feta, broken into small chunks

For the dressing
6 tbsp extra-virgin olive oil
Juice of ½ lemon
2 tbsp torn fresh mint
2 tbsp chopped fresh flatleaf parsley
1 small garlic clove, crushed
Pinch of sugar

1. Preheat the oven to 240°C/fan 220°C/gas 9. Line a baking sheet with baking paper and place the tomatoes on top, cut-side up. Drizzle with 1 tablespoon of the olive oil and sprinkle with salt and freshly ground black pepper. Roast for 15 minutes. Reduce the oven temperature to 150°C/fan 130°C/gas 2 and roast for a further 1¼–1½ hours, until they have shrivelled in size and are lightly browned around the edges but still juicy in the centre. Leave to cool.

2. Meanwhile, drizzle the remaining tablespoon of oil over the courgettes, season and cook on a hot griddle or in a frying pan for 2 minutes each side, until lightly charred. Leave to cool. In a large salad bowl, mix together the courgettes, cucumber, onion, olives and salad leaves.

3. Whisk together the ingredients for the dressing and season well.

4. Just before serving, add the feta, tomatoes and dressing to the salad and toss together gently. Divide among 4 plates to serve.

★DELICIOUS. TIP If time is a little tight, look out for semi-dried, mi-cuit or SunBlush tomatoes in your local supermarket or deli, and use instead of the slow-roasted tomatoes.

Greek beef burger with beetroot relish

This quick burger recipe provides a wonderful taste of sunny Greece.

SERVES 4
READY IN 30 MINUTES

500g best-quality beef mince

1 tbsp dried oregano (Greek, if possible)

Small bunch of flatleaf parsley, finely chopped

Small handful of fresh mint leaves, finely chopped

60g feta, cubed

50g rocket leaves

4 poppy seed rolls, lightly toasted

4 tbsp mayonnaise, to serve (optional)

For the beetroot relish:

200g cooked beetroot, cubed

3 small pickled onions, finely chopped

2 tbsp green olives, pitted and roughly chopped

1 tbsp chopped fresh mint

1. Mix all the relish ingredients together in a small bowl. Season with salt and pepper, and set aside.

2. Put the beef mince in a bowl, season and mix in the dried oregano, parsley and mint. With wet hands, form into 4 burgers, then press a few cubes of feta into the centre of each and press the mince back over to reshape and cover the cheese completely. Cover and chill for up to 12 hours, if you wish. Otherwise, light your barbecue, or preheat the grill to Medium.

3. Barbecue or grill the burgers for 3–4 minutes, turning halfway, until cooked through.

4. Place some rocket on each roll, top with a burger and some relish. Serve with mayonnaise, if you like.

Prawn and avocado quinoa salad

Quinoa (pronounced *keen-wa*) is a tiny grain from South America with a lovely texture and mild flavour. It also absorbs other flavours really well, especially herby and citrus ones.

SERVES 4
READY IN 25 MINUTES

100g quinoa

15g butter

2 garlic cloves, finely chopped

350g raw prawns, tail-shells on

250g ripe tomatoes, cut into wedges

Small bunch of fresh dill, chopped

Small bunch of fresh flatleaf parsley, chopped

6 spring onions, finely sliced

1 large ripe avocado, halved, stoned, peeled and sliced

50g Kalamata olives, pitted and chopped

2 tbsp extra-virgin olive oil, plus extra for drizzling

Juice of 1 lemon

1. Place the quinoa in a large pan and cover with water. Bring to the boil and cook for 20 minutes, until tender. Drain well and set aside.

2. Meanwhile, heat the butter in a large frying pan, add the garlic and prawns, and cook for 3 minutes, until the prawns are cooked through.

3. Place the prawns in a large bowl and stir in the tomatoes, dill, parsley, onions, avocado, olives, extra-virgin olive oil and the lemon juice. Stir in the drained quinoa and season well to taste.

★ DELICIOUS. TIP If you want to barbecue the prawns, cook them on the grate before stirring them into the quinoa.

Cumberland sausage rings with sweet tomato relish

Everyone loves sausages at a barbecue, but these coiled ones are easy to cook and taste great with the sweet, herby relish.

SERVES 12
TAKES 20 MINUTES, PLUS ABOUT
40–50 MINUTES ON THE BARBECUE

2kg small Cumberland sausage rings or unlinked sausages (see tip below)

Oil, for brushing

For the sweet tomato relish:

3 tbsp olive oil

1 large onion, chopped

2 garlic cloves, crushed

500g vine-ripened tomatoes, roughly chopped

100g sun-dried tomatoes in olive oil, drained and chopped

2 tbsp tomato purée

2 tbsp clear honey

2 tbsp chopped fresh oregano or thyme

1. Light your barbecue. To coil your own sausages, cut the single length into three. Tightly coil each piece into a spiral and then push a couple of long metal skewers through each one to keep them in shape and make them easier to turn during cooking.

2. Make the relish. Heat the oil in a sturdy frying pan set over the hot barbecue bars (or a medium heat on a hob). Add the onion and garlic, and fry for 6–8 minutes, until lightly browned. Add the remaining ingredients and cook for 10–15 minutes, stirring, until reduced and thickened. Season and keep warm.

3. Brush the sausage rings with oil and barbecue directly over a medium heat for 10–12 minutes, turning halfway, until nicely browned. Turn off the middle burner or rearrange the coals to either side of the grate and cook for a further 5–6 minutes on each side, until cooked through.

4. Cut the sausage rings into wedges and serve with the relish and crusty bread.

★ DELICIOUS. TIP If you can't buy Cumberland rings, get a long length of unlinked sausages in natural casings from your butcher, then twist it into a ring. If you have a pack of sausages, untwist them at the joins and squeeze the sausagemeat into the gaps to make one long length.

Pancetta-wrapped tomato, courgette and Emmental tart

This tortilla-like tart is attractive, tasty, and makes a striking centrepiece for an al fresco feast for friends.

SERVES 6
TAKES 40 MINUTES, PLUS 50 MINUTES IN THE OVEN, PLUS COOLING

Olive oil, for greasing
18 thin slices pancetta
500g medium-sized new potatoes, thinly sliced
4 large eggs
4 tbsp double cream
125g Emmental, grated
2 tbsp chopped fresh thyme leaves, plus extra to garnish
2 tbsp chopped fresh flatleaf parsely
2 tbsp snipped fresh chives
2 small courgettes, sliced
2 ripe tomatoes, sliced

1. Preheat the oven to 180°C/fan 160°C/gas 4. Line the base and sides of an 18cm-round, 4cm-deep, loose-bottomed tin with baking paper, then oil. Arrange the pancetta slices over the base and up the sides of the tin, overlapping slightly.

2. Cook the potato slices in a pan of boiling water for 3 minutes, until just tender. Drain and pat dry. Arrange them over the base of the tin, overlapping slightly, and press down well.

3. Beat together the eggs, cream and some seasoning. Ladle a third of the egg mixture over the potatoes and scatter with a third of the cheese and chopped herbs. Arrange half the courgette slices on top, and repeat.

4. Arrange the tomato slices and remaining courgette slices on top. Ladle over the remaining egg mix and scatter with the remaining cheese and chopped herbs.

5. Bake for 50 minutes, until just set – cover with foil if browning too much. Cool for 20 minutes. Serve warm or cold, cut into wedges, scattered with fresh thyme.

Tuna, cannellini bean and red onion salad on tomato bread

This is ideal for eating outdoors in the summer, a wonderful lunchtime dish, or served in smaller portions as a starter.

SERVES 4
READY IN 20 MINUTES

400g can or jar cannellini beans, drained and rinsed

300g jar good-quality tuna in olive oil, drained and flaked into large chunks

1 small red onion, finely sliced

12 cherry tomatoes, halved

Large handful of fresh flatleaf parsley leaves, roughly chopped

3 tbsp olive oil

2 small lemons

1 tsp Dijon mustard

1 garlic clove, crushed or grated

4 thick slices sourdough or rye bread

3 tbsp sun-dried tomato paste

1. In a large bowl, mix together the beans, tuna, red onion, tomatoes and parsley.

2. In another bowl, whisk together 2 tablespoons of the olive oil, the juice of 1 lemon, and the mustard and garlic. Season, pour over the tuna and beans and toss together well.

3. Heat a griddle pan until very hot. Brush the bread on both sides with the remaining oil and griddle for 1 minute each side, until golden with charred lines.

4. Spread one side with the tomato paste. Pile on the beans and tuna, and serve with the remaining lemon, cut into wedges, to squeeze over.

★ DELICIOUS. TIP It's important to get really good tuna from a deli for this dish, as it is the main ingredient in this recipe and will be well worth the little extra expense.

smart food for special occasions

Roast rib of beef with watercress, Roquefort and walnut salad

Roast beef doesn't have to be kept for the cold winter months; it also makes a splendid summer dish, served with salad.

SERVES 6

TAKES 45 MINUTES, PLUS ABOUT
1½–2 HOURS IN THE OVEN AND
20 MINUTES RESTING

3kg 2-bone beef fore-rib, chined (ask your butcher to prepare this cut for you)
Beef dripping or olive oil

For the salad:
1 large red onion, cut into thin wedges
5 tsp olive oil
1 mini French stick, cut into thin slices
½ tsp Dijon mustard
1 tbsp balsamic vinegar
4 tbsp extra-virgin olive oil
2 x 85g bags watercress sprigs, large stalks removed
150g Roquefort, crumbled
75g walnut halves, lightly toasted

1. Preheat the oven to 240ºC/fan 220ºC/gas 9. Weigh the beef and calculate the cooking time at 12–13 minutes per 500g for rare, or 17–18 minutes per 500g for medium, plus 15 minutes. Rub with dripping or oil, season, place in a roasting tin and roast for 15 minutes, until well browned. Lower the oven temperature to 190ºC/fan 170ºC/gas 5 and cook for the remaining calculated cooking time. Lift the beef on to a board, cover with foil and leave to rest for 20 minutes.

2. Meanwhile, make the salad. While the beef is roasting at the lower temperature, toss the onion wedges with 2 teaspoons of the oil in another roasting tin. Roast for 20–25 minutes alongside the beef, turning once, until soft and just browned.

3. Fry the bread slices in the remaining oil for 2–3 minutes each side until golden. Drain on kitchen paper.

4. Whisk the mustard with the vinegar, then gradually whisk in the extra-virgin olive oil. Season.

5. Carve the beef. Toss the watercress in a bowl with half the dressing. Add the onion, croutons, cheese and nuts, and toss together. Serve with the beef and the remaining dressing.

Grilled sea bass on garlic mash with lemon and chive butter sauce

The lemon and chive butter sauce perfectly complements the delicate flavour of the sea bass in this smart suppertime dish.

SERVES 4
READY IN 45 MINUTES

100g butter
2 sea bass (about 500–750g),
  scaled and filleted
2 tbsp snipped fresh chives
Finely grated zest of ¼ lemon,
  plus the juice of ½ lemon
Steamed green vegetables,
  to serve

For the garlic mash:
1kg floury potatoes, cut into
  large chunks
4 garlic cloves, peeled
25g butter
2 tbsp full-cream milk

1. First make the mash. Put the potatoes into a pan of salted water with the garlic. Bring to the boil and simmer for 20 minutes, until tender.

2. Meanwhile, preheat the grill to High. Melt the butter in a pan over a low heat. Brush the fish fillets on both sides with some of the melted butter, season and put skin-side up on the rack of the grill pan.

3. Drain the potatoes and garlic, then pass through a potato ricer back into the pan, or mash until smooth. Stir in the butter, milk and seasoning. Keep warm.

4. Grill the fish fillets for 5–6 minutes, until the skin is lightly browned and the fish cooked through.

5. Stir the chives, lemon zest and juice into the remaining butter in the pan.

6. Divide the mash among four plates and rest the fish alongside. Spoon over the butter and serve with some steamed green vegetables.

Pan-fried pork noisettes with green peppercorn sauce

Pork tenderloin is the ideal cut for this quick and tasty French recipe.

SERVES 4
READY IN 20 MINUTES

2 x 450g pork tenderloins (fillets)
50g butter
25g plain flour
150ml dry white wine
150ml chicken stock
300ml whipping cream
1 tsp Dijon mustard
Squeeze of fresh lemon juice
2–3 tsp green peppercorns in brine, drained and rinsed
Boiled or mashed potatoes, to serve

1. Trim the pork tenderloins of any fat and membrane, then slice each one across, slightly on the diagonal, into 2cm thick slices (noisettes).

2. Melt the butter in a large, heavy-based frying pan. Season the noisettes, then coat lightly in the flour, patting off the excess. As soon as the butter is foaming, add the noisettes and cook over a medium–high heat for 3–4 minutes on each side, until browned and cooked through. Lift on to a plate, cover and keep warm.

3. Pour the fat away, place the pan over a high heat and add the wine and stock. Boil rapidly until reduced by three-quarters (to about 75ml). Add the cream and mustard, and boil for a further 3–4 minutes until reduced to a light coating sauce consistency. Add the lemon juice and green peppercorns, and season to taste.

4. Return the pork to the pan just to warm through. Serve with boiled or mashed potatoes.

Variation Change the amount of green peppercorns, according to your taste, or use some coarsely crushed black pepper instead.

Quails with pomegranate

This dish has its roots in the Middle East, where poultry is braised in a sauce of pomegranates and walnuts. This version is lighter and quicker, but equally delicious.

SERVES 4
READY IN ABOUT 30 MINUTES,
PLUS 3–4 HOURS MARINATING

8 quails (2 per person)
15g butter
1 tbsp olive oil
1 pomegranate
75ml sherry or white wine
A simple leaf salad, some bread and Greek-style yogurt, to serve

For the marinade:
1 tbsp olive oil
Juice of 2 lemons
2 bay leaves
2 garlic cloves, roughly chopped
½ tsp crushed black pepper

1. Combine all the marinade ingredients in a large bowl, add the quails, cover and marinate in the fridge for 3–4 hours.

2. Preheat the oven to its highest setting. Heat a heavy-based frying pan over a medium–high heat, add the butter, olive oil and the quails, and brown on all sides. Transfer to a roasting tin, pour over the marinade and roast for 20 minutes or until the juices run clear.

3. While the birds are roasting, cut the pomegranate in half and bash the skin side with a spoon to remove the seeds.

4. Remove the quails from the oven and drain the cooking juices back into the frying pan. Bring to the boil over a high heat, add the sherry or wine and pomegranate seeds, and simmer until glossy. Pour back over the quails and serve with a simple leaf salad like chicory or watercress, some bread and some Greek-style yogurt on the side.

Oriental roast chicken with coconut gravy

In this roast, a simple blend of oriental spices, lime and herbs is used to flavour the inside and outside of the bird, as well as the gravy.

SERVES 4
TAKES 20 MINUTES, PLUS
1½ HOURS ROASTING

1 tbsp vegetable oil
2 tsp Thai spice blend or
  Chinese five spice powder
½ tsp coarse salt
Grated zest and juice of 1 lime,
  plus 1 extra lime, halved
1.5kg whole free-range chicken
2 lemongrass stalks, bruised
4 thick slices fresh root ginger
2 fresh or dried lime leaves
200g carton coconut cream
200ml chicken stock, hot
1 tbsp Thai red curry paste
Steamed greens and rice,
  to serve

1. Preheat the oven to 200°C/fan 180°C/gas 6. Mix together the oil, spice blend or five spice, salt, lime zest and juice to make a paste. Rub the mixture evenly on to the chicken skin.

2. Pop the lime halves into the body cavity, along with the lemongrass, ginger and lime leaves. Place in a roasting tin and roast for 1½ hours, until the chicken is cooked through. Tip any juices from inside the body cavity into the tin, then lift the chicken on to a plate and rest for 5 minutes.

3. Meanwhile, pour off the fat from the tin, stir in the coconut cream, stock and curry paste and cook in the oven for a further 5 minutes, until hot. Carve the chicken and serve with the coconut gravy and some steamed greens, such as pak choi, and rice.

Seared salmon with cucumber, ginger and hot chilli salsa

Cool cucumber and fresh mint are the perfect foil for the raging heat of red chillies in this quick yet elegant recipe.

SERVES 4
READY IN 20 MINUTES

1 small or ½ large cucumber

2 red chillies, halved, seeded and finely chopped

Small handful of fresh flatleaf parsley leaves, chopped

Small handful of fresh mint leaves, chopped

1 tbsp grated fresh root ginger

4 skinned salmon fillets (about 200–250g each)

Splash of olive oil

250g tub crème fraîche

1. Halve and seed the cucumber, then cut the flesh into small dice. Put into a bowl and stir in the chopped chillies, parsley, mint, ginger and some seasoning. Set aside.

2. Brush the salmon fillets on both sides with olive oil. Heat a little oil in a large frying pan and sear the salmon for 2–3 minutes on each side until just tender and cooked through. Divide among four plates. Spoon a dollop of crème fraîche on each, then top with the hot chilli salsa.

Garlic squid and prawns with black linguine

This dish is a universal favourite, and the simplicity of it lies in the timing – the moment the pasta is ready, so is the sauce!

SERVES 4
READY IN 15 MINUTES

400g prepared small squid (ask your fishmonger to clean them for you)

300g squid ink or regular linguine

4 tbsp extra-virgin olive oil, plus extra for drizzling

300g large peeled raw prawns, tail-shells on

4 garlic cloves, finely chopped

1 bunch of spring onions, trimmed and sliced

300g baby tomatoes, halved

50g bag fresh wild rocket

Juice of 1 lemon

1. Cut along one side of each squid pouch and open them out flat. Using a small, sharp knife, score the inner sides in a diamond pattern, then cut the flesh into 5cm pieces. Set aside with the tentacles.

2. Cook the linguine in salted boiling water for 8 minutes or until al dente. Drain, reserving a little of the cooking liquid.

3. Heat the oil in a large frying pan over a high heat. Add the squid and stir-fry for 2 minutes or until golden and lightly caramelised. Lift out and set aside. Add the prawns, garlic and spring onions, and cook for 2 minutes. Add the tomatoes and cook for a further 1–2 minutes or until the prawns are cooked through. Add the squid and toss lightly.

4. Stir the rocket and a splash of the reserved cooking liquid through the linguine. Add the seafood mixture, lemon juice and seasoning, and toss once more. Divide among four bowls, drizzle with a little oil, and serve.

Roast guinea fowl with lemon and rosemary and sweet-and-sour gravy

This simple yet sophisticated roast would be just perfect served with some parsnip mash and broccoli sautéd with garlic.

SERVES 6
READY IN 1 HOUR 10 MINUTES

2 guinea fowl (about 1kg each)
6 fresh rosemary sprigs
4 garlic cloves
2 lemons, halved

For the sweet-and-sour gravy:
50g butter, at room temperature
1 tbsp olive oil
500g shallots, halved
Leaves of 1 fresh rosemary sprig, finely chopped
75ml balsamic vinegar
600ml fresh chicken stock, hot
1 tbsp plain flour

1. Preheat the oven to 190°C/fan 170°C/gas 5. Season the birds inside and out, then push 3 rosemary sprigs and 2 garlic cloves inside each one and place in a roasting tin. Squeeze over 1 lemon, then stuff the squeezed and un-squeezed halves inside each cavity. Loosely cover the tin with foil.

2. Roast in the oven for 30 minutes. Uncover and roast for 20–30 minutes more until cooked through. Transfer to a platter, cover with foil and leave to rest.

3. Meanwhile, make the gravy. Heat half the butter and the oil in a pan over a low heat. Add the shallots, cover and cook, stirring occasionally, for 30 minutes. Uncover and cook for 15 minutes until tender and caramelised. Add the rosemary, cook briefly, then add the vinegar and simmer vigorously until syrupy. Add the stock and simmer for 10 minutes until reduced slightly. Mix the remaining butter with the flour, whisk into the sauce and simmer until thickened. Season and keep warm.

4. Transfer the birds to a board and joint each one into 10 pieces. Divide among warmed plates, and serve with the gravy.

Variation Use a couple of small free-range chickens in place of the guinea fowl, if you prefer.

Basil and lime salmon

This quick and easy salmon with lime and basil couldn't be easier to make – and will keep all your guests satisfied.

SERVES 10

TAKES 20 MINUTES, 30–40 MINUTES BAKING, PLUS COOLING AND CHILLING

- 1 whole salmon (about 2.5kg), filleted and skinned to give 2 large fillets
- Juice and finely grated zest of 4 limes, plus 1 lime, thinly sliced, to serve
- 250g garlic and herb soft cheese
- 8 tbsp ready-made hollandaise sauce from a jar
- 20 fresh basil leaves, chopped, plus extra sprigs to serve

1. Preheat the oven to 190°C/fan 170°C/gas 5. Lay a large sheet of foil in the base of a large roasting tin. Top with a sheet of non-stick Teflon. Put a salmon fillet on top, skinned-side down and season. Squeeze over the lime juice.

2. Mix together the soft cheese, hollandaise sauce, chopped basil and lime zest. Spoon on top of the salmon fillet. Top with the other fillet, skinned-side up, and wrap in the Teflon sheet and foil. Bake for 30–40 minutes until just cooked through. Leave wrapped up to cool, then chill in the fridge until needed.

3. To serve, scrape away the brown flesh from the top of the salmon, then carefully transfer the fillets to a serving platter. Garnish with lime slices and basil. Cut into chunky slices to serve.

★ DELICIOUS. TIP You can make this up to 2 days in advance, making it perfect for entertaining. Make up to the end of step 2, then cover and chill until needed.

Pan-fried duck breasts with sour cranberry sauce

Fruit always goes well with the richness of duck, and here the acidity of the cranberries is a welcome contrast.

SERVES 4
TAKES 50 MINUTES, PLUS
OVERNIGHT SOAKING

4 x 175–200g duck breasts

For the sour cranberry sauce:
75g dried cranberries
**300ml red wine, such as
  Cabernet Sauvignon**
25g white sugar
1 tbsp red wine vinegar
¾ tsp arrowroot

1. Put the duck breasts on a plate and cover loosely with greaseproof paper (this dries out the skin and helps to make it crispy), then chill overnight. At the same time also soak the dried cranberries in the red wine and leave overnight.

2. The next day, put the sugar into a small pan with 1 tablespoon of cold water and heat gently until the sugar dissolves. Then boil vigorously to form an amber-coloured caramel. Take off the heat, add the vinegar, return to the heat and add the cranberries and wine. Simmer for 20 minutes. Mix the arrowroot with 2 tablespoons of water, stir in and simmer for 1 minute. Season and keep warm.

3. Lightly score the skin of each breast with a diamond pattern, then season. Heat a dry, heavy-based frying pan over a high heat. Add the duck, skin-side down, lower the heat to medium and cook for 3–4 minutes until crisp and golden. Turn and cook for 5 minutes. Lift on to a board and rest for 5 minutes. Then slice and serve with the sauce.

Risotto cakes

These elegant savoury rice cakes can be made well in advance and fried just before serving, making them ideal for stress-free entertaining.

SERVES 4
TAKES AROUND 45 MINUTES, PLUS COOLING

1 tbsp olive oil
50g butter
1 onion, finely chopped
½ tsp saffron strands
300g arborio or carnaroli risotto rice
150ml dry white wine
1 litre fresh vegetable or chicken stock
75g Parmesan, grated
Seasoned flour
Poached eggs and crispy pancetta, to serve

1. Heat the olive oil and half the butter in a wide, non-stick pan over a medium heat. Add the onion and cook, stirring, for 5 minutes, until softened. Stir in the saffron until it begins to release its colour, then add the rice. Stir for 1 minute to coat in the butter, then pour in the wine and bubble until absorbed.

2. Meanwhile, put the stock in a small saucepan and bring to a low simmer. Add a ladleful to the rice, stirring until absorbed. Continue adding the stock one ladleful at a time, stirring frequently, for about 20 minutes until the rice is creamy and tender, but still al dente.

3. Stir in the remaining butter and Parmesan, cover and leave to cool.

4. Divide the mixture into 8 and shape into cakes. Dip in seasoned flour, then pan-fry in oil over a medium heat for 3–4 minutes on each side, until golden and hot throughout. Serve topped with a poached egg and some crispy pancetta.

Variation You could flavour these cakes in many ways. For example, use dolcellate instead of Parmesan and add chopped herbs, diced cooked ham or cooked peas.

Salad of smoked duck, dried cranberries and spiced pecans

This salad could be served as either a summery main course or a smart starter for a special meal.

SERVES 8
READY IN 20 MINUTES

35g shelled pecan nuts
15g butter
½ tsp ground mixed spice
1 tbsp soft dark brown sugar
2 x 85g bags watercress
2 red chicory, leaves separated
75g dried cranberries, soaked in boiled water for 5 minutes, drained
200g sliced smoked duck breast

For the dressing:
½ tsp Dijon mustard
1½ tbsp red wine vinegar
3 tbsp olive oil
4½ tbsp hazelnut oil
1 tsp crème de cassis

1. Put the nuts into a hot, dry frying pan over a medium heat and toast for about 30 seconds. Add the butter, mixed spice and sugar, reduce the heat slightly and cook for 1½–2 minutes, turning halfway. The nuts should be caramelised, but be careful not to let them burn. Season, then spread out on a baking sheet to cool.

2. Meanwhile, make the dressing. Put the mustard and vinegar in a small bowl, then whisk in the oils. Add the crème de cassis in two stages, so you can check for sweetness. Season.

3. In a bowl, toss the watercress, chicory, cranberries and spiced nuts with most of the dressing. Divide among plates, arrange the duck on top and drizzle with the rest of the dressing.

Wild mushroom, mascarpone and tarragon torte

Try to leave this tart to cool for 10 minutes before serving, because then the delicate flavours are easier to taste.

SERVES 6
TAKES 30 MINUTES, 45–50 MINUTES BAKING, PLUS CHILLING

350g chilled shortcrust pastry
1 large red onion, very thinly sliced
Large pinch of caster sugar
1 tbsp extra-virgin olive oil
45g butter
500g mixed wild and chestnut mushrooms, trimmed and thinly sliced
25g mascarpone
100ml double cream
2 large eggs, beaten
50g Parmesan or Grana Padano, finely grated
1 tbsp chopped fresh tarragon
2 tbsp chopped fresh flatleaf parsley

1. Preheat the oven to 200°C/fan 180°C/gas 6. Roll the pastry out thinly and use to line a 23cm-round x 4cm-deep, loose-bottomed flan tin. Chill for 20 minutes.

2. Line the pastry with baking paper and beans, and bake for 15 minutes. Remove the paper and beans, and bake for a further 5 minutes.

3. Meanwhile, fry the onion and sugar in a frying pan with the oil and 15g of the butter until soft and caramelised. Season and tip into a bowl.

4. Melt another 15g of the butter in the frying pan, add half the mushrooms and cook over a high heat for 2–3 minutes, until any excess moisture has evaporated. Season and add to the onion. Repeat. Cool slightly.

5. Beat the mascarpone and cream together until smooth, then mix in the eggs, half the cheese, the mushrooms, herbs and some seasoning. Spoon into the pastry case and scatter with the remaining cheese. Bake for 25–30 minutes, until golden. Serve warm with a salad.

Variation Tarragon goes extremely well with the flavour of mushrooms, but if it is not one of your favourite herbs, use some chopped fresh thyme leaves instead.

on the side

Zesty bulgur wheat tabbouleh

Bulgur wheat has been de-husked, parboiled, dried and then cracked into coarse pieces. Its nutty flavour is wonderful in salads like this.

SERVES 6
READY IN 20 MINUTES

200g bulgur wheat
1 cucumber, peeled, seeded and diced
6 medium tomatoes, diced
Bunch of spring onions or 1 small red onion, finely chopped
Large bunch of fresh flatleaf parsley, finely chopped
Large bunch of fresh mint, chopped
1 garlic clove, finely chopped
3 tbsp olive oil
Juice of 1 large lemon

1. Place the bulgur wheat in a large bowl and pour over boiling water until just covered. Cover with a clean tea towel and stand for 15 minutes, until tender. Drain the bulgur wheat well and place in a sieve. Squeeze out the excess water using a spoon.

2. Place the cucumber, tomatoes, onions and herbs in a large bowl and toss together well. Add the drained bulgur wheat, garlic, olive oil and lemon juice, and season well to taste. This goes very well with griddled or barbecued chicken served with a wedge of lemon.

Greek salad

This classic recipe, redolent of Greece, has a real taste
of summer.

SERVES 6
READY IN 20 MINUTES

1 head cos lettuce

1 cucumber, halved lengthways,
  seeded and diced

1 large onion, thinly sliced

6 plum tomatoes, cut into
  chunks

24 pitted Greek black olives,
  halved

225g feta, diced

For the dressing:

2 tbsp fresh lemon juice

6 tbsp extra-virgin olive oil

1 garlic clove, crushed

2 tbsp chopped fresh oregano
  or thyme

1. Separate the lettuce leaves and tear them into
bite-sized pieces. Wash and dry well. Put the
cucumber, onion, tomatoes, olives and feta into a
bowl, add the lettuce and toss together briefly.

2. Put the ingredients for the dressing together
in a glass jar, seal and shake vigorously until they
are well mixed. Pour over the Greek salad just
before serving.

Potato salad with radishes

This easy potato and radish salad is very refreshing and perfect as part of a buffet or barbecue.

SERVES 10, AS PART OF A BUFFET
READY IN 25 MINUTES

2kg waxy new potatoes, such as Charlotte, halved if large
2 bunches radishes, trimmed and finely sliced
Bunch of spring onions, finely sliced
2 punnets mustard cress, trimmed

For the dressing:
5cm piece fresh horseradish, finely grated or 2 tbsp creamed horseradish
Juice of ½ lemon
4 tbsp olive oil
2 tbsp mayonnaise

1. Bring a large pan of salted water to the boil and add the potatoes. Simmer for 15–20 minutes, or until tender. Drain and tip into a large serving bowl.

2. Mix the dressing ingredients in a bowl and pour over the potatoes. Season, toss together and leave to cool.

3. Add the radishes, spring onions and cress to the potatoes and gently toss together.

Five spice coleslaw

If you think coleslaw is 'rabbit' food, think again. This one,
delicately flavoured with five spice, sesame oil and lime, is a
little bit different and just as delicious.

SERVES 6
READY IN 20 MINUTES

½ **white cabbage, thinly sliced**
2 **carrots, finely shredded**
Bunch of radishes, thinly sliced
½ **cucumber, halved, seeded**
  and thinly sliced
6 **spring onions, shredded**

For the dressing:
4 **tbsp light mayonnaise**
1 **tsp sesame oil**
Juice of 1 lime
1 **tsp Chinese five spice**

1. Put the cabbage, carrots, radishes, cucumber
and spring onions into a large bowl. Cover and chill
until ready to serve.

2. Mix all the dressing ingredients together in a
bowl and season to taste with salt and pepper. Toss
with the coleslaw ingredients just before serving.

Variation Following the oriental theme, you
could try substituting the white cabbage with
shredded kohlrabi, another crunchy, green
member of the cabbage family.

Green bean and sesame seed salad

The flavours in this unusual bean salad are irresistible.

SERVES 6
READY IN 15 MINUTES

500g fine green beans, trimmed
Small bunch of fresh mint
Small bunch of fresh flatleaf parsley
1 tsp white wine vinegar
1 tbsp olive oil
2 tbsp sesame seeds, toasted
1 small red onion, very finely chopped

1. Cook the green beans in a large saucepan of boiling water for 4–5 minutes, until tender. Drain well.

2. Meanwhile, place the mint and flatleaf parsley in a small food processor and whiz until finely chopped. Add the vinegar and olive oil and some salt and pepper, and whiz again briefly, until combined.

3. Tip the warm green beans into a bowl. Add the herb dressing, along with the sesame seeds and red onion, and toss together well. Set aside to cool, then cover and chill until you are ready to serve.

Orange and watercress salad

This zingy salad would go wonderfully with some barbecued or griddled chicken.

SERVES 4–6
READY IN 15 MINUTES

4 oranges, preferably navel or Valencia
6 spring onions
175g watercress
2 chicory heads, broken into leaves
6 tbsp extra-virgin olive oil

1. Using a small, sharp knife, take a thin slice off the top and bottom of each orange. Stand the oranges on a chopping board and cut away the skin and pith, working from top to bottom, in sections. Hold an orange in one hand over a bowl and cut along either side of the membrane to remove each segment, letting each segment and the juice fall into the bowl. Repeat for all the oranges. Strain off and reserve the juice. Put the segments into a serving bowl.

2. Trim the spring onions, halve and finely shred lengthways. Add to the orange segments with the watercress and chicory.

3. Put 2 tablespoons of the orange juice into a small bowl and whisk in the oil and plenty of seasoning. Just before serving, drizzle the dressing over the salad and toss everything together.

Red cabbage and beetroot salad

Red cabbage often gets overlooked in favour of the white, coleslaw-style variety, but it makes especially crunchy, colourful salads too.

SERVES 4
READY IN 15 MINUTES

3 plump garlic cloves, crushed
1 tbsp Dijon mustard
1 tbsp red wine vinegar
3 tbsp extra-virgin olive oil
450g raw baby beetroot
100g finely shredded red
  cabbage
1 small bunch of spring onions,
  trimmed and shredded
2 tbsp chopped fresh flatleaf
  parsley
1 tbsp poppy seeds

1. Put the garlic, mustard and vinegar into a bowl and whisk well. Gradually whisk in the olive oil and season generously. Set aside.

2. Peel the beetroot and grate using a grater or food processor. Put into a bowl with the shredded cabbage and spring onions, parsley and poppy seeds. Drizzle over the dressing and toss together using two forks.

Courgette, fennel, potato and lemon salad

This is another great barbecue dish, which makes a lovely accompaniment to a summer roast of lamb or chicken.

SERVES 4–6
TAKES 20 MINUTES, PLUS
30 MINUTES STANDING

50ml extra-virgin olive oil, rapeseed oil or sunflower oil

Finely grated zest and juice of 2 lemons (unwaxed, if possible)

6 small courgettes, topped and tailed

1 fennel bulb, cored and very thinly sliced, any leaves reserved to garnish

3 medium waxy potatoes

Rustic bread, to serve

1. In a large bowl, combine the oil, lemon zest and juice with a good pinch of sea salt to make a thin dressing.

2. Using a wide vegetable peeler, peel the courgettes lengthways into thin strips. Add to the dressing along with the fennel and fold everything together so that the dressing covers all the vegetables. (The lemon juice and salt will slightly 'cook' the courgettes and soften them up.) Leave this mix to stand for a good 30 minutes, stirring halfway.

3. Meanwhile, cut the potatoes into bite-sized pieces. Boil in plenty of salted boiling water for about 8–10 minutes or until they are just tender but in no danger of falling apart. Drain thoroughly and set aside to cool slightly.

4. Toss the warm potatoes with the courgette and fennel mixture, and season with black pepper. Divide among plates, garnish with any reserved fennel leaves and serve with plenty of rustic bread to mop up the dressing.

Variation You could use yellow courgettes instead of green ones, and baby fennel if you can get it. The younger the courgettes are, the better they will taste.

Creamy potato and onion gratin

This easy-to-make gratin would be the perfect partner for almost any roast – beef, chicken, pork or lamb.

SERVES 4–6
TAKES 20 MINUTES, PLUS
1¼ HOURS IN THE OVEN

40g butter, melted, plus extra for greasing
1.3kg floury potatoes, such as Maris Piper
1 red onion, thinly sliced into rounds
1 fresh bay leaf
284ml carton double cream

1. Preheat the oven to 190°C/fan 170°C/gas 5. Grease a deep 2-litre baking dish with butter.

2. Peel and thinly slice the potatoes, placing them in a bowl of water to prevent discolouring. Drain, then pat dry with a clean tea towel. Arrange with half the onion slices in the dish, overlapping them, seasoning and drizzling with the melted butter as you go. Finish the top layer neatly with the remaining onion. Top with a bay leaf, then pour over the cream.

3. Cover the dish with foil, place on a baking sheet and bake in the oven for 45 minutes. Uncover and bake for a further 30 minutes, until tender and golden.

Variation This would also be wonderful topped with a little coarsely grated cheese before baking. Go for a hard, tasty one, such as Cheddar or Gruyère.

Braised peas and carrots, French-style

This fresh and tasty side dish is ideal to serve with any fish or meat dish, particularly roast chicken.

SERVES 6–8
READY IN 20 MINUTES

25g butter
Small bunch of spring onions, finely sliced
450g Chantenay or baby carrots, halved lengthways
200ml fresh vegetable stock
450g frozen peas
1 romaine lettuce, shredded

1. Melt the butter in a large, wide saucepan over a medium heat. Add the sliced spring onions and cook for 2–3 minutes, until softened. Add the carrots and vegetable stock, and stir well. Bring to the boil, then reduce the heat, cover and simmer for 4 minutes.

2. Add the peas and lettuce, return to the boil and cook for a further 4 minutes, or until the carrots are tender. Season to taste and serve.

Variation You could also use freshly shelled peas when they are in season instead of frozen. They are lovely with a little chopped fresh mint stirred in at the end.

Griddled vegetables and feta couscous

This is wonderful as a side dish, but could be served as a veggie main course, perhaps with griddled halloumi cheese.

SERVES 4
READY IN 30 MINUTES

250g wholegrain couscous (see tip below)

1 courgette, cut lengthways into thin slices

1 aubergine, cut lengthways into thin slices

2 red peppers, seeded and cut into long thin slices

3 tbsp olive oil

1 tbsp cumin seeds

1 tbsp fennel seeds

Juice of 1 large lemon

1 large red chilli, seeded and finely chopped

50g pine nuts, toasted

50g dried sour cherries (from major supermarkets)

150g feta, crumbled into pieces

Handful of fresh coriander, chopped

Tub of fresh houmous, to serve

1. Place the couscous in a large bowl and pour over boiling water until just covered. Cover with a clean tea towel and leave for 5 minutes or until the couscous has absorbed the water. Fluff up the grains with a fork.

2. Heat a griddle pan until hot. Place the courgette, aubergine and peppers in a large bowl, and toss with 2 tablespoons of the olive oil and the cumin and fennel seeds until all the vegetables are coated. Place the vegetables on the griddle pan, a few at a time, and griddle for 2 minutes each side, until charred and softened.

3. Stir the griddled vegetables into the couscous along with the remaining olive oil, lemon juice, chilli, pine nuts and sour cherries.

4. Fold in the feta and coriander, and season well. Serve with the houmous.

★ DELICIOUS. TIP Look out for wholegrain couscous as it has a great nutty taste and texture and holds its shape better in salads than regular couscous. It's readily available in all major supermarkets.

Cauliflower gratin

Cauliflower gratin often gets overlooked in favour of other vegetable side dishes, but this dish here is excellent with any roasted or grilled meats.

SERVES 6
READY IN 50 MINUTES

1 large cauliflower, trimmed but some green leaves left attached
500ml full-cream milk
1 small onion, halved
1 tsp black peppercorns
2 fresh bay leaves
2 large pieces of blade mace
30g butter
30g plain flour
4 tbsp double cream
3 tbsp finely grated mature Cheddar

1. Cut the green leaves off the cauliflower and reserve, then break the head into large florets. Put the milk, onion, peppercorns, bay leaves and mace into a non-stick pan over a medium heat. Bring to the boil, then set aside for 30 minutes to infuse.

2. Bring the milk back to the boil, then strain into a jug. (Discard the solids.) Put the butter in a clean pan and melt over a low heat. Stir in the flour and cook for 30 seconds. Gradually add the hot milk and bring to the boil, stirring until thickened. Remove from the heat, stir in the cream and season.

3. Preheat the grill to High. Cook the cauliflower and green leaves in a pan of boiling water for 4 minutes or until just tender. Drain and transfer to a large, shallow ovenproof dish. Pour over the sauce, sprinkle with the cheese and grill for 2–3 minutes until lightly golden.

Stir-fried cabbage with cumin, chilli and lemon

This unusual way of cooking cabbage is a real winner.

SERVES 4
READY IN 15 MINUTES

2 tsp cumin seeds
1 tbsp groundnut or
  vegetable oil
¼ tsp dried chilli flakes
1 pointed green cabbage,
  halved, cored and shredded
25g butter, softened
Juice of 1 small lemon

1. Heat a large, deep frying pan over a medium–high heat. Add the cumin and dry-fry until lightly toasted. Tip into a bowl.

2. Add the oil to the pan and when it is hot, add the chilli and cabbage. Stir-fry for 4–5 minutes, until just wilted but still a little crunchy. Add the butter, toasted cumin seeds and lemon juice, and toss through. Season, then serve.

delicious
desserts

Vanilla bean and white chocolate panna cotta

These delicate little creams are ideal for summer entertaining, especially served with soft seasonal berries, such as raspberries.

SERVES 4
TAKES 30 MINUTES, PLUS
OVERNIGHT CHILLING

500ml single cream
1 tbsp vanilla bean paste
50g white vanilla chocolate, broken up
3 sheets leaf gelatine
Fresh berries, to serve

1. Heat the cream in a pan over a medium heat. When it just begins to boil, reduce the heat and stir in the vanilla paste and chocolate. Whisk until the chocolate has melted, then remove from the heat.

2. Soak the gelatine in cold water for 10 minutes, until softened, then lift out and squeeze out the excess. Put 4 tablespoons of boiling water in a bowl, add the gelatine and stir to melt. Add the cream mixture, mix and pour equal amounts into 4 x 150ml moulds (dariole moulds or small yogurt pots would be ideal). Chill overnight.

3. Dip the moulds briefly in hot water and invert on to plates. Decorate with fresh berries, and serve.

Double espresso tart

The flavours of both chocolate and coffee work wonderfully together and no more so than in this elegant, but enticing, creamy custard tart.

SERVES 12
TAKES 1½ HOURS, PLUS 3–4 HOURS
TO SET

250g digestive biscuits
2 tbsp cocoa powder
125g butter, melted
2 egg yolks
100g caster sugar
1 tbsp cornflour
600ml milk
3 sheets of leaf gelatine
200g plain chocolate, about 70% cocoa solids, broken into pieces
150g plain chocolate, about 50% cocoa solids, broken into pieces
2 tbsp finely ground espresso coffee grains
284ml carton double cream
Few chocolate curls, to decorate

1. Crush the biscuits into fine crumbs. Place in a bowl, and stir in the cocoa powder and melted butter. Press the mixture over the base and up the sides of a 20cm-round springform cake tin. Chill for at least 30 minutes.

2. Mix the egg yolks, sugar, cornflour and 4 tablespoons of the milk together in a bowl. Soak the gelatine leaves in cold water for 10 minutes until softened.

3. Heat the remaining milk in a pan over a low heat. Add the chocolates and the espresso grains, stirring until the chocolate has melted. Then stir into the egg mixture, return to the pan over a low heat and stir until thickened and smooth.

4. Lift the gelatine out of the water, squeeze out any excess water then add to the hot custard and stir until it has dissolved. Cool for 15 minutes, then pour into the biscuit base. Allow to cool, then chill for 3–4 hours until set. Whip the cream until thick, spoon over the top of the tart and decorate with chocolate curls.

★ DELICIOUS. TIP Don't worry about the fine coffee grains going into the smooth tart – they give it a really nice texture.

Caramel orange pavlovas

Easy marshmallow-like meringues and oranges dripping with gooey caramel make perfect partners in this decadent dessert.

SERVES 6
TAKES 30 MINUTES, 45 MINUTES
IN THE OVEN, PLUS COOLING

3 large egg whites
175g caster sugar
1 tsp cornflour
½ tsp white wine vinegar
284ml carton double cream

For the caramel oranges:
175g caster sugar
2 tbsp orange-flavoured
  liqueur, such as Cointreau
3 large oranges

1. Preheat the oven to 140°C/fan 120°C/gas 1. Line a large baking sheet with non-stick baking paper. Whisk the egg whites and a pinch of salt into stiff peaks. Slowly whisk in the sugar to form a glossy meringue. Whisk in the cornflour and vinegar. Drop 6 large tablespoonfuls on to the baking sheet and shape each into an 8cm round with a dip in the centre. Bake for 45 minutes. Turn off the oven and leave them inside to cool.

2. Make the caramel oranges. In a small pan, dissolve the sugar in 4 tablespoons of water, then boil rapidly to form a rich, amber-coloured caramel. Plunge the base of the pan into cold water, then add the liqueur and 5 tablespoons of water and return to a low heat. Stir until the caramel has dissolved. Leave to cool. Segment the oranges, drain away any juice and spoon 4 tablespoons of the caramel over them.

3. Whip the cream, spoon on to each pavlova and top with the caramel oranges. Drizzle with more caramel to serve.

★ DELICIOUS. TIP The pavlovas, caramel and orange segments can be done the day before. Store the pavlovas in an airtight container, the caramel in a screw-top jar and the oranges covered in a bowl in the fridge.

Mango puddings with chilli syrup

A touch of chilli might sound odd, but it adds a little subtle heat to these light and fruity baked puddings.

SERVES 6
TAKES 35 MINUTES, PLUS
25 MINUTES BAKING

175g self-raising flour, plus extra for dusting
175g butter, softened, plus extra for greasing
½ ripe mango, peeled, stoned and thinly sliced
1 tsp baking powder
175g golden caster sugar
3 large eggs, beaten
2 tbsp milk
Finely grated zest of 2 limes

For the chilli syrup:
Pared zest of 1 lime and juice of 2
100g golden caster sugar
3 red bird's eye chillies

1. Make the chilli syrup. Add water to the lime juice to make a quantity of 150ml. Put into a pan with the pared lime zest, sugar and chillies, and bring to the boil, stirring. Simmer for 10 minutes. Remove and reserve the chillies and lime zest, and set aside with the syrup.

2. Preheat the oven to 200°C/fan 180°C/gas 6. Place a square of baking paper into the base of 6 x 150ml pudding basins. Dust each with flour. Lightly grease 6 x 12cm squares of foil and fold a pleat into the centre of each. Arrange the mango slices in the base of each basin and drizzle with a teaspoon of syrup.

3. Sift the flour and baking powder into a bowl, and add the butter, sugar, eggs, milk and grated lime zest. Beat for 2 minutes until smooth. Spoon into the basins and cover tightly with the foil. Place in a roasting tin, then pour in boiling water to come halfway up the sides of the basins. Bake for 25 minutes.

4. Unmould the puddings on to a serving platter, spoon over a little chilli syrup and decorate with the reserved chillies and lime zest. Serve with crème fraîche.

★ DELICIOUS. TIP The reserved chillies are for decoration, not eating, as they are very, very hot.

Variation If chilli for pudding is not your thing, flavour the syrup with a couple of star anise instead.

Pears in quince syrup

This dessert is stylish yet very simple. Perfect for a gathering of good friends.

SERVES 6
READY IN 30 MINUTES

100g quince cheese
1 vanilla pod
6 dessert pears
Small Italian biscotti and
crème fraîche, to serve

1. Put the quince cheese and 500ml boiling water in a wide, deep pan over a medium–low heat. Heat for a few minutes, until the quince cheese has melted.

2. Split open the vanilla pod and scrape the seeds into the quince syrup. Add the pod to the pan, too. Peel and core the pears, add to the syrup and bring to a simmer. Cover and cook for 5–10 minutes or until the pears are tender – they are ready when a skewer is easily inserted into their centres.

3. Using a slotted spoon, remove the poached pears from the quince syrup and put into a serving dish. Season the syrup with freshly ground black pepper, then pour all over the pears, discarding the vanilla pod.

4. Serve the pears while warm or at room temperature with small Italian biscotti and crème fraîche.

★ DELICIOUS. TIP Serve with good-quality vanilla ice cream instead of crème fraîche, if you prefer.

Praline meringue stacks

This impressive-looking recipe might seem time-consuming, but it's worth it – stacks of praline meringue and boozy cream, topped with crunchy praline pieces.

SERVES 6
TAKES 45 MINUTES, PLUS 35 MINUTES
BAKING, PLUS COOLING

75g caster sugar
40g whole blanched hazelnuts
40g whole blanched almonds
Vegetable oil, for greasing

For the meringue:
2 large egg whites
Pinch of cream of tartar
50g caster sugar
35g icing sugar, sifted
142ml carton double cream
1 tbsp Frangelico (hazelnut
  liqueur), Tia Maria or Baileys

1. Dissolve the sugar in a pan over a medium–low heat. Increase the heat slightly and cook until it forms a rich, amber-coloured caramel. Quickly stir in the nuts, then immediately tip out on to a lightly oiled baking sheet. Set aside to cool.

2. Break half the cooled praline into a food processor and whiz to a fine powder. Set aside with the remaining praline.

3. Preheat the oven to 150°C/fan 130°C/gas 2. Mark 18 x 6cm circles on to three sheets of baking paper. Turn the paper over and use to line three large baking sheets.

4. For the meringue, whisk the egg whites and cream of tartar to soft peaks. Gradually whisk in the caster sugar to form a stiff meringue. Fold in the icing sugar and praline powder. Spoon into a large piping bag fitted with a 1cm plain nozzle. Pipe in a spiral on to each marked circle. Bake for 35 minutes, until pale golden. Leave to cool.

5. Whip the cream and liqueur to soft peaks. Sandwich the meringues together with the cream. Roughly chop the remaining praline and use to decorate. Serve immediately.

★ DELICIOUS. TIP The meringues and praline will keep in an airtight box in a cool place for up to 3 days, ready to assemble for serving.

Caramelised pecan tart

A rich, nutty tart that is delicious served with scoops of
vanilla ice cream.

SERVES 8–10

TAKES 15 MINUTES, PLUS ABOUT
1 HOUR IN THE OVEN, PLUS CHILLING

375g chilled shortcrust pastry

300g pecan nut halves, broken
into pieces

150g runny honey

120g unsalted butter

100ml double cream

2 tbsp bourbon or whiskey

5 medium egg yolks

150g golden caster sugar

1 tsp vanilla extract

1 tsp grated fresh nutmeg

1. Roll out the pastry thinly on a lightly floured
surface and use to line a 24–25cm x 4cm-deep
round loose-bottomed flan tin. Prick the base with
a fork and chill for 20 minutes.

2. Preheat the oven to 200°C/fan 180°C/gas 6.
Line the pastry case with greaseproof paper and
baking beans. Bake blind for 15 minutes. Remove
the paper and beans, and bake for a further
5 minutes, until the pastry is pale golden.
Remove and lower the oven temperature to
190°C/fan 170°C/gas 5.

3. Spread the pecans over a baking sheet and
lightly toast in the oven for 5–6 minutes. Remove
and set aside.

4. Put the honey, butter, cream and bourbon or
whiskey in a pan, and warm briefly until the butter
has melted. Beat the egg yolks in a bowl, then
stir in the honey-syrup mixture, pecans, sugar,
vanilla extract, nutmeg and a pinch of salt. Pour
the mixture into the pastry case and bake for
40 minutes. Serve warm or cold, cut into wedges,
with scoops of ice cream.

Sparkling summer fruit jellies

These summer fruit jellies fizz with sparkling white wine and glorious fruity flavours. Make them in attractive tall glasses for maximum effect.

MAKES 6
TAKES 10 MINUTES, PLUS COOLING
AND CHILLING

135g raspberry jelly, broken up into cubes

475ml Prosecco or champagne

200g mixed fresh summer berries, such as strawberries, raspberries, blackcurrants and blackberries, hulled and halved if necessary

142ml carton single cream, to serve

Fresh mint leaves, to decorate

Crisp sweet biscuits, to serve

1. Put the jelly cubes in a jug, pour over 100ml boiling water and stir until the jelly has dissolved. Cool, then slowly stir in the Prosecco – you should have about 600ml liquid.

2. Divide the fruit among 6 x 150ml pretty glasses, then pour some of the jelly into each, just to cover the fruit. Cover and chill until the surface is just set – this holds the fruit in place so that it doesn't float to the surface.

3. Top up with the remaining jelly, cover and chill until set.

4. Pour the cream on to each jelly in a thin layer, then decorate with fresh mint leaves. Serve with crisp, sweet biscuits, such as vanilla shortbreads.

★ DELICIOUS. TIP You can make these up to 2 days ahead. Cover and chill until serving.

Blackberry and apple cranachan

The combination of whipped cream, crunchy oats, fresh fruit and blackberry liqueur here is simply divine.

SERVES 4
READY IN 30 MINUTES

50g butter
75g rolled oats
50g caster sugar
150ml whipping cream
115g Greek yogurt
2 tbsp each honey, whiskey, and light muscovado sugar
200g blackberries
2 tart apples, such as Granny Smith, peeled, cored and sliced
Crème de mûre or crème de cassis, to drizzle
Shortbread, to serve (optional)

1. Melt half the butter in a small pan, add the oats and cook for 1 minute. Then add half the caster sugar and stir for 4–5 minutes, until the oats are lightly caramelised. Tip on to a piece of baking paper and leave to cool.

2. Lightly whip the cream, then fold in the yogurt, honey, whisky, muscovado sugar and oats. Lightly crush most of the blackberries (set aside a few to decorate), and gently fold in.

3. In a pan, melt the remaining butter and sauté the apples (in 2 batches, if necessary) for 3–4 minutes. When the apples begin to soften, add the remaining caster sugar and cook until caramelised.

4. Layer up the cream mixture with the apples in 4 glasses or 1 big bowl. Top with the reserved blackberries and drizzle with a little crème de mûre or cassis. Serve with shortbread, if you like.

★ DELICIOUS. TIP You can use Bramley apples instead of Granny Smith, if you like, but dip them in sugar before sautéing.

Dorset apple cake

There are as many versions of this cake as there are cooks, but this lemony one is wonderful. Serve with clotted cream

SERVES 8
TAKES 25 MINUTES, PLUS 1 HOUR
BAKING, PLUS COOLING

**225g butter, softened, plus
  extra for greasing**
450g Bramley apples
**Finely grated zest and juice of
  1 lemon**
**225g caster sugar, plus extra
  for dredging**
3 large eggs
225g self-raising flour
2 tsp baking powder
25g ground almonds
1 tbsp demerara sugar
Clotted cream, to serve

1. Preheat the oven to 180°C/fan 160°C/gas 4. Grease a deep, 23–24cm-round, springform cake tin and line with baking paper. Peel, core and cut the apples into 1cm pieces, and toss with the lemon juice.

2. Beat together the butter, caster sugar and lemon zest in a bowl until pale and fluffy. Beat in the eggs, one at a time, adding a little flour with each egg.

3. Sift the remaining flour and the baking powder into the bowl, and fold in with the ground almonds. Drain the apple pieces well, then stir into the mixture. Spoon into the prepared tin, lightly level the top and sprinkle with the demerara sugar. Bake for 1 hour or until a skewer inserted into the centre of the cake comes out clean. If the cake starts to look too brown, cover with a sheet of baking paper after about 45 minutes.

4. Leave the cake to cool in the tin for 10 minutes, then remove and dredge heavily with the extra caster sugar. Cut into wedges and serve warm with clotted cream.

Variation Though it's not traditional in Dorset, firm pears, such as Conference would also work well in this pudding.

Cheesecake cups with fresh raspberry sauce

These individual cheesecakes topped with fresh raspberries are a real winner in the summer.

MAKES 9

TAKES 25 MINUTES, PLUS CHILLING AND COOLING

100g plain chocolate (70% cocoa solids), broken up
40g unsalted butter
250g digestive biscuits, crushed
300g cream cheese
6 tbsp icing sugar
142ml carton double cream
Juice of 1 orange
250g fresh raspberries, plus extra to decorate

1. Line a muffin tin with 9 paper muffin cases. Melt the chocolate and butter into a pan over a low heat. Remove from the heat and stir in the crushed biscuits. Press the mixture evenly on to the base and up the sides of each paper case to make a shell. Chill for 15 minutes.

2. For the cheesecake filling, put the cream cheese and 4 tablespoons of the icing sugar in a bowl and whisk until smooth – don't use an electric hand whisk. Add the cream and continue to whisk, gradually adding 2 tablespoons of the orange juice, until soft peaks form. Divide among the cases and chill for 1 hour.

3. Meanwhile, put the raspberries in a pan with the remaining icing sugar and orange juice. Stir over a medium heat, to dissolve the icing sugar, then simmer for 2–3 minutes. Pass through a sieve and discard the pips. Leave to cool and thicken slightly.

4. Top each cheesecake cup with some extra raspberries and spoon over the raspberry sauce to serve.

Spicy apple and pear crumbles with blackberry cream

These are a clever way of serving a traditional nursery pud in style.

SERVES 4

TAKES 30 MINUTES, PLUS 20 MINUTES IN THE OVEN

450g cooking apples, peeled, cored and sliced

2 firm dessert pears, such as Conference, peeled, cored and sliced

Finely grated zest of 1 lemon

100g golden caster sugar

75g butter

175g plain flour

½ tsp mixed spice

50g light muscovado sugar

50g lightly roasted hazelnuts, coarsely chopped

A little demerara sugar, to decorate

For the blackberry cream:

150g fresh blackberries

2 tsp golden caster sugar

1 tbsp crème de cassis (optional)

2 tsp fresh lemon juice

300ml double cream

1. Preheat the oven to 200°C/fan 180°C/gas 6. Gently cook the prepared fruit, lemon zest and caster sugar in a covered pan for 7–8 minutes until just tender. Tip into a sieve set over a bowl and leave to drain.

2. Rub the butter into the flour. Stir in the spice and 1 tablespoon of the muscovado sugar. Place four buttered 10cm cooking rings on to a greased baking sheet. Spoon 2 heaped tablespoons of the crumb mixture into each. Press down lightly to make a base, then spoon over the fruit mixture. Reserve the syrup.

3. Stir the remaining muscovado sugar and the hazelnuts into the remaining crumble. Spoon on top of the fruit and bake for 20 minutes.

4. Meanwhile, make the blackberry cream. Set aside 8 blackberries. Put the remainder into a bowl with the sugar, crème de cassis, if using, and lemon juice. Crush lightly. In another bowl, whip the cream to soft peaks, then fold in the blackberries.

5. Transfer the crumbles to plates and remove the rings. Sprinkle with a little demerara sugar. Decorate with the remaining blackberries, and serve with the reserved syrup and blackberry cream.

Individual summer puddings

These puddings are a real taste of summer with their mix of raspberries, blackcurrants and redcurrants.

MAKES 4

TAKES 30 MINUTES, PLUS COOLING
AND OVERNIGHT CHILLING

250g raspberries

125g blackcurrants, picked from the stalks

125g redcurrants, picked from the stalks

100g caster sugar

6 thin slices white bread, crusts removed

2 tbsp crème de cassis, plus extra to serve

Single cream, to serve

1. Put the fruit and sugar in a pan over a medium heat. Gently simmer for 3–4 minutes, stirring occasionally, until the sugar has dissolved and the juices have begun to run from the fruit. Don't overcook the fruit; you want it to retain its shape and freshness. Remove from the heat and cool slightly.

2. Using a 6cm plain cutter, cut out four rounds from 2 slices of the bread (keep the trimmings). Dip both sides into the fruit, so the juices soak the bread, then use to line the base of 4 x 150ml individual pudding basins.

3. Tear the remaining bread into pieces and stir into the fruit mixture, along with the crème de cassis. Spoon into each mould and cover with cling film. Place on a baking sheet and weigh each one down – full pots of yogurt are ideal. Chill overnight.

4. The next day, run a knife around each pudding to loosen, then turn out on to serving plates. Drizzle with extra crème de cassis and serve with cream.

Amaretti tortoni with brandy snaps and raspberries

These simple yet glamorous individual ice creams can be made well ahead of time, making them ideal for entertaining.

SERVES 6–8
TAKES 30 MINUTES, PLUS
6–7 MINUTES IN THE OVEN, PLUS
FREEZING AND COOLING

142ml carton single cream
284ml carton double cream
2 egg whites
3 tbsp dark rum or sweet
  sherry
30g caster sugar
75g amaretti biscuits or
  macaroons, coarsely crushed
Brandy snaps, raspberries and
  icing sugar, to serve

1. Put both creams and the egg whites into a large bowl, and whisk vigorously using an electric hand whisk for about 8 minutes, until the mixture forms soft peaks. Whisk in the rum or sherry, then gradually whisk in the sugar. Gently fold in the crushed biscuits.

2. Divide the mixture among six individual souffle dishes (8cm diameter x 5.5cm deep) or 225ml ramekins. Cover with cling film and freeze for 8 hours until firm or for up to 1 month.

3. To serve, remove the tortoni from the freezer and leave them to soften very slightly at room temperature for 15 minutes. Dip each dish briefly in hot water, then turn out on to plates. Arrange the brandy snaps on top and the raspberries alongside. Dust with icing sugar and serve.

★ DELICIOUS. TIP If you don't have individual moulds, freeze the tortoni in a 1-litre loaf tin, then slice to serve. Serve any leftover brandy snaps with coffee after a meal on another day.

Note: This recipe contains raw egg.

Menu planners

Seared scallops on pea and mint risotto (page 38)

★

Roast guinea fowl with lemon and rosemary (page 112)
Braised peas and carrots, French-style (page 144)
Creamy potato and onion gratin (page 142)

★

Caramel orange pavlovas (page 158)

CASUAL DINNER FOR 6

Fish pie with cheesy leek mash topping (page 46)

★

Braised peas and carrots, French-style (page 144)

★

Blackberry and apple cranachan (1½ x recipe, page 170)

SUNDAY LUNCH FOR 4

Coronation prawn and mango cocktail (page 22)

★

Crispy crackling roast pork with roasted apples and
sage and onion stuffing (page 42)

Creamy potato and onion gratin (page 142)

Stir-fried cabbage with cumin, chilli and lemon
(page 150)

★

Spicy apple and pear crumbles with blackberry cream
(page 176)

AUTUMNAL VEGETARIAN SUPPER FOR 6

Kabocha squash soup with pumpkin seed pesto
(page 30)

★

Oven-baked porcini mushroom and taleggio rice
(1½ x recipe, page 64)

Green bean and sesame seed salad (page 134)

★

Pears in quince syrup (page 162)

Menu planners

MAKE-AHEAD SUPPER FOR 6

Buttered sea trout and prawn pots with dill and soda
bread (page 28)

★

Roasted Mediterranean vegetable lasagne (page 56)

A mixed leaf salad

Garlic bread

★

Amaretti tortoni with brandy snaps and raspberries
(page 180)

FAR-EASTERN DINNER PARTY FOR 6

Thai fish cakes on lemongrass sticks (page 14)

★

Indonesian beef rendang (page 58)

Cucumber, tomato, red onion and coriander salsa/salad

Steamed rice

★

Mango puddings with chilli syrup (page 160)

187

Index

Picture and recipe credits

Harper Collins would like to thank
the following for providing
photographs:

Steve Baxter p13, p15, p17, p31,
p57, p71, p75, p77, p79, p85, p99,
p101, p129, p131, p137, p139, p151,
p173; Peter Cassidy p37, p45, p59,
p83, p111, p123, p159, p167, p177,
p181; Stephen Conroy p143, p161;
Rob Fiocca p65; Ewen Francis
p155; Jonathan Gregson p27, p33,
p89, p127, p141, p146, p149, p171;
Richard Jung p35, p113, p121,
p165; Emma Lee p81, p91; Gareth
Morgans p61; Lis Parsons p19, p21,
p25, p29, p53, p87, p93, p133, p135,
p163, p169; Michael Paul p43, p49,
p55, p103, p109, p115, p117, p157,

p175, p179; Craig Robertson p67,
p73, p95; Deidre Rooney p105;
Lucinda Symons p63, p145; Philip
Webb p23, p39, p47, p107; Rob
White p51, p119

With thanks, too, for the following
for creating the recipes for
delicious. which are used in
this book:

Kate Belcher p12, p34, p50, p118,
p142, p174, p178; Angela Boggiano
p44, p88, p92, p94, p126, p130,
p146, p148; Angela Boggiano and
Alice Hart p66; Lorna Brash p114;
Sally Clarke p24, p168; Matthew
Drennan p52, p74, p76, p78, p108,
p128, p136, p138, p144, p156, p164;

Silvana Franco p72, p106, p132,
p134; Alice Hart p86; Diana Henry
p120, p170; Catherine Hill p84,
p110, p160; Debbie Major p18, p20,
p22, p28, p30, p36, p38, p42, p46,
p54, p56, p58, p64, p70, p80, p82,
p90, p98, p100, p102, p116, p122,
p150, p158, p166, p172, p176, p180;
David Morgan p14, p16; Kim
Morphew p162; Tom Norrington-
Davies p26, p32, p104, p140; Carol
Tennant p62, p112; Linda Tubby
p154; Marcus Wareing p48; Mitzie
Wilson p60